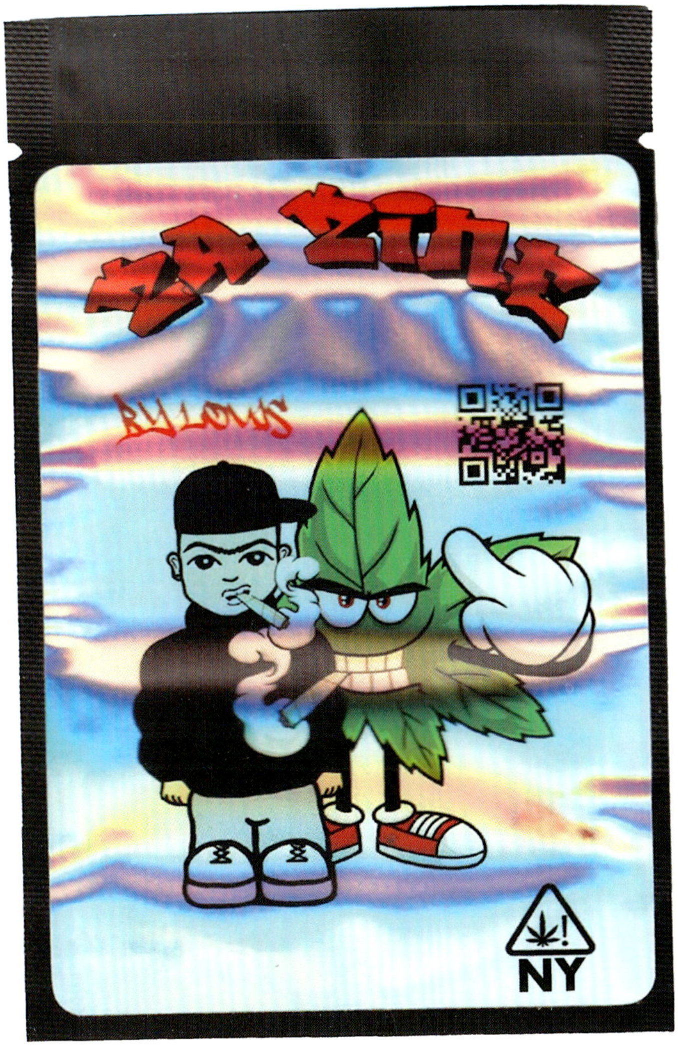

za zine

A collection of weed bags found in New York City

November 2023 to February 2024

By Louis, 2024

The purpose of this publication is not to glamorize drug use, but to present the history of a subculture through its relics.

We at Blurring Books feel moved by the Japanese concept known as 'mono no aware' which translates to 'a sensitivity of ephemera'. The ephemera in this book documents artifacts of a time in our shared history and offers commentary on consumer culture.

foreword

In 2021 after recreational marijuana was legalized in New York, an onslaught of guerilla smoke shops that sold weed began opening all over the city, beating any state-sanctioned dispensaries to the market. Almost overnight, it felt like every empty storefront was a smoke shop and every deli had added weed to their inventory. In an immediately over saturated market with accessibility like never before, the question of how to make your product stand out arose. The answer? Branding!

This shift from black market to commercial led to an unprecedented emphasis on visuals for the weed being purchased, a renaissance of sorts. Never before seen strains whose names and designs played on current events, pop culture, lifestyles, luxuries and vices started showing up everywhere while more traditional strains like Sour Diesel or Gorilla Glue suddenly garnered an infinite amount of new visual interpretations. Soon enough, these bags were littered all over the streets and it became clear that they were, in most cases, unrelated to the strain of weed inside and served mostly as a visual aid - like a trading card.

These bags are notably original and inventive - gaudy, sexy and masculine in the same way AXE Body Spray is. With seemingly endless variations of subject matter that felt completely unique to this moment of New York history, they've become their own artistic medium. Za Zine is a collection of these bags that I found in New York City between November 2023 and February 2024.

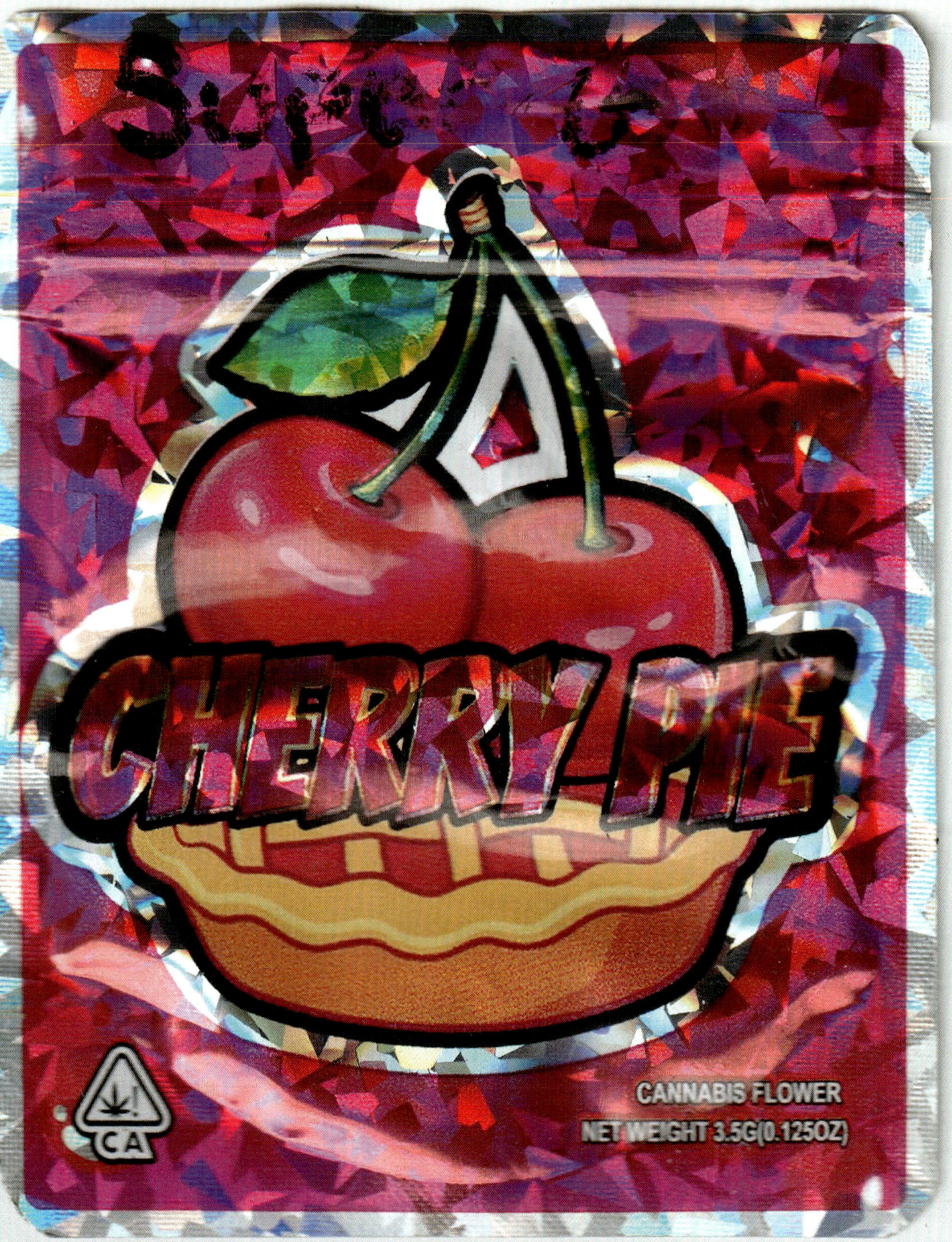
CHERRY PIE
CANNABIS FLOWER
NET WEIGHT 3.5G(0.125OZ)
CA

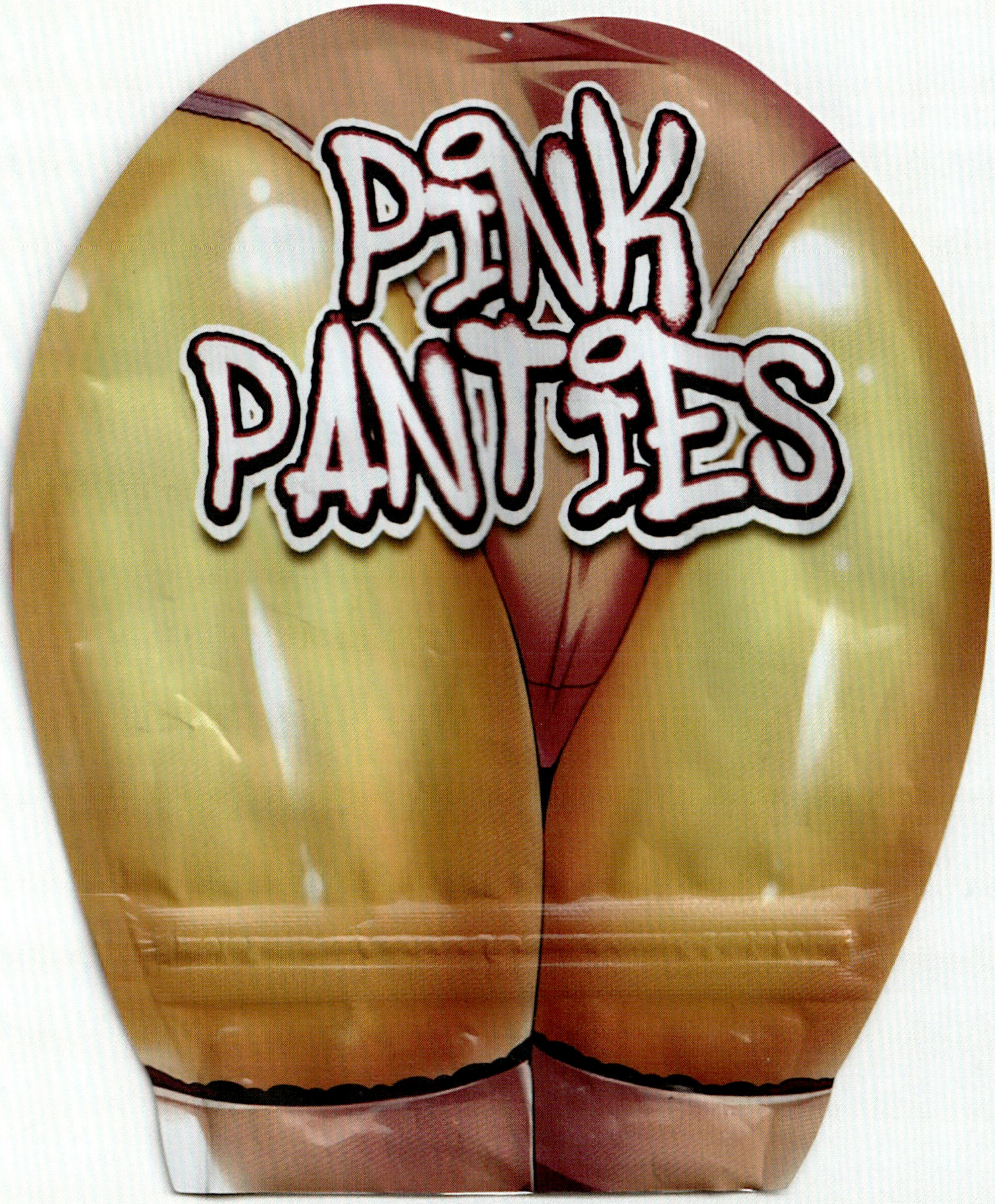
PINK
PANTIES

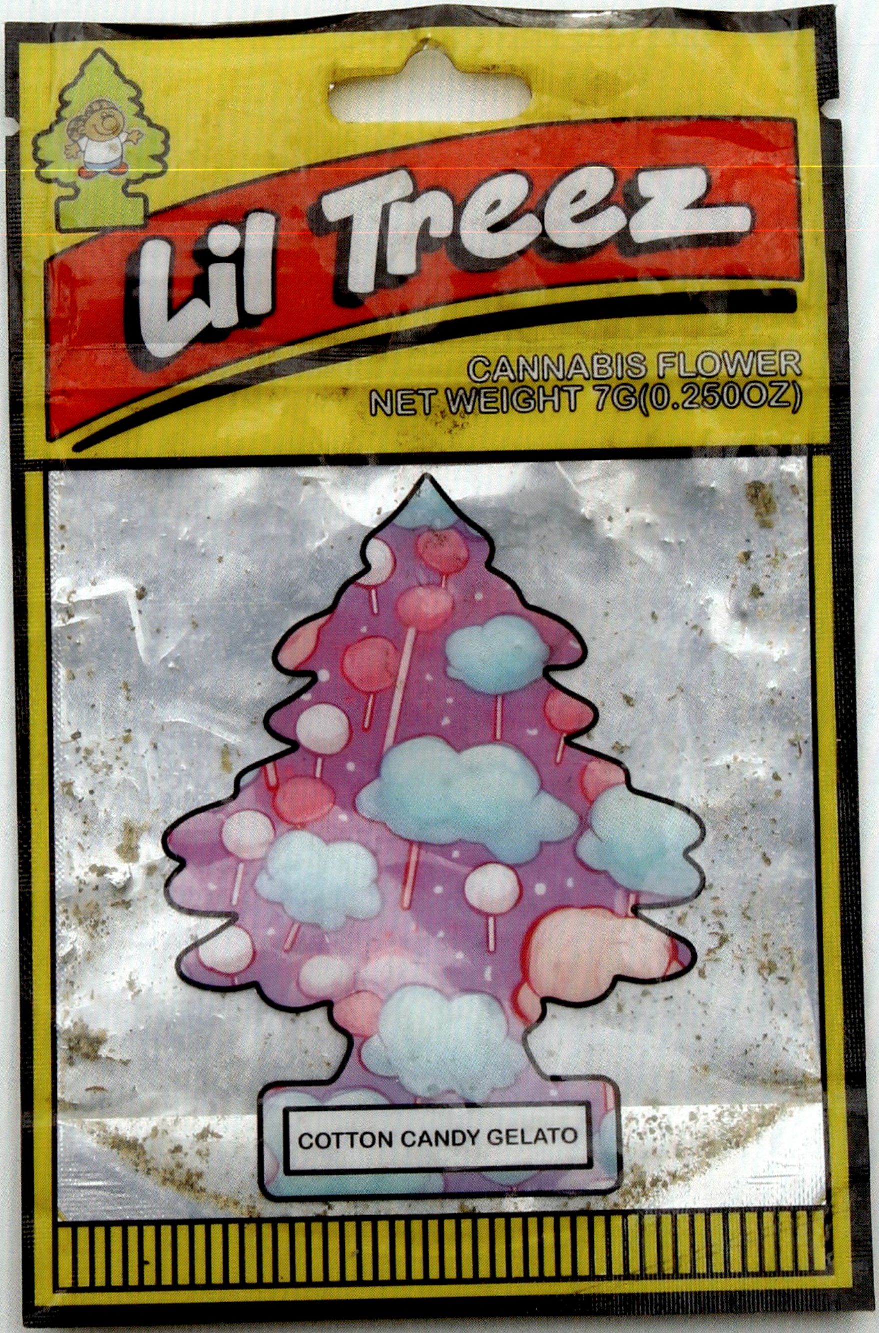
Lil Treez
CANNABIS FLOWER
NET WEIGHT 7G(0.250OZ)
COTTON CANDY GELATO

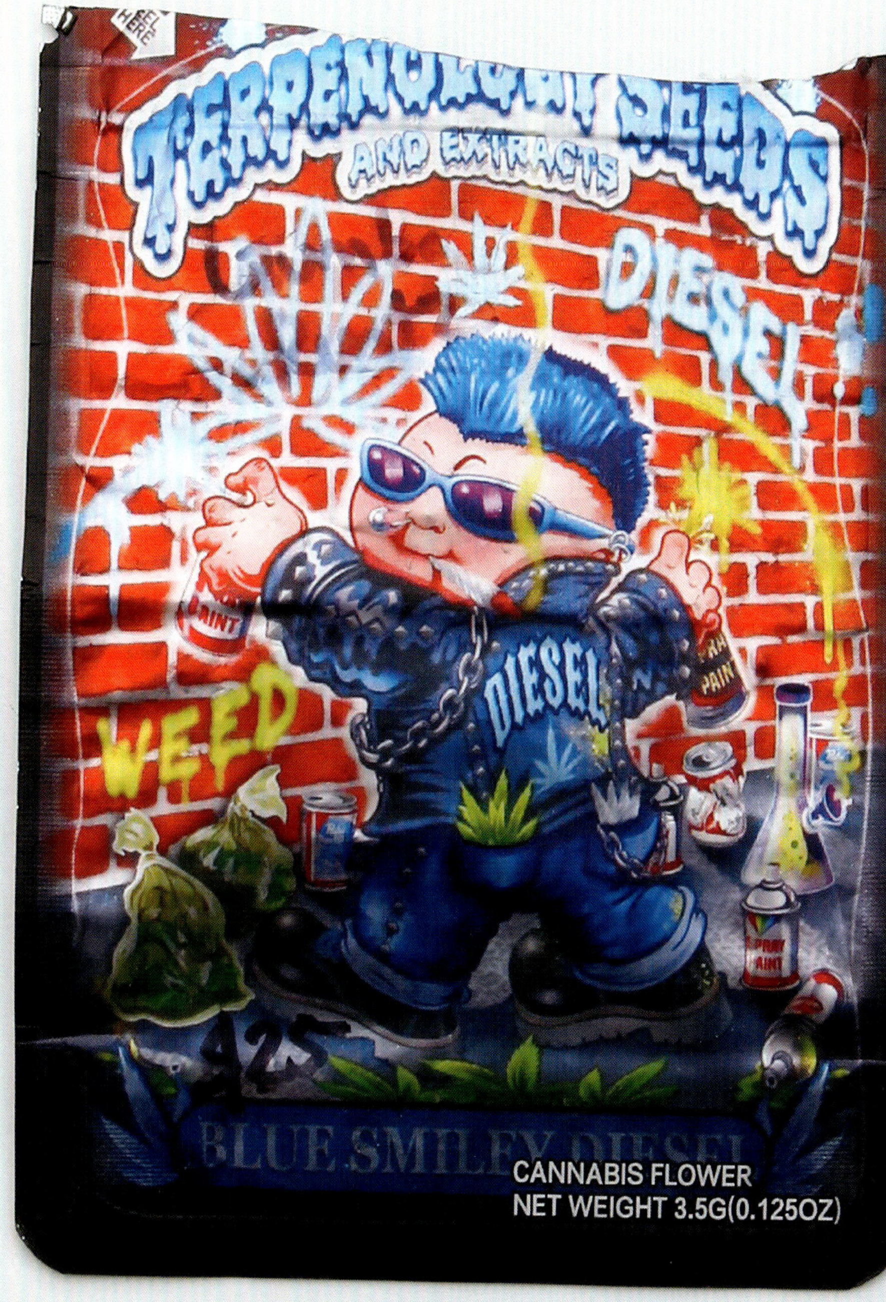
AND EXTRACTS
DIESEL
DIESEL
WEED
CANNABIS FLOWER
NET WEIGHT 3.5G(0.125OZ)

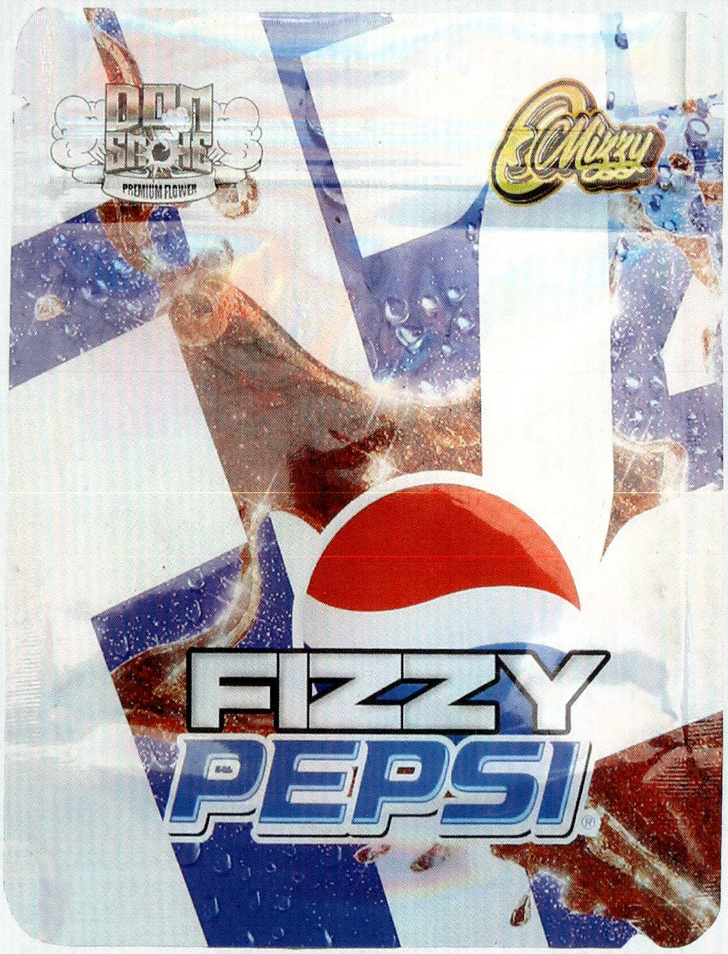
PREMIUM FLOWER
FIZZY
PEPSI

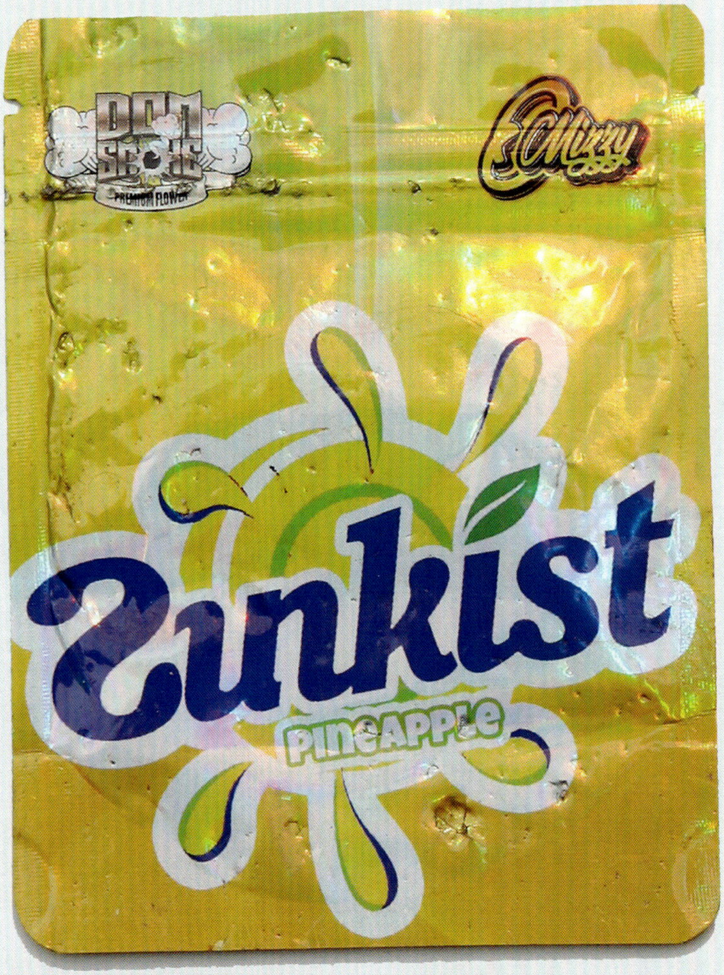
PREMIUM FLOWER
Zunkist
PINEAPPLE

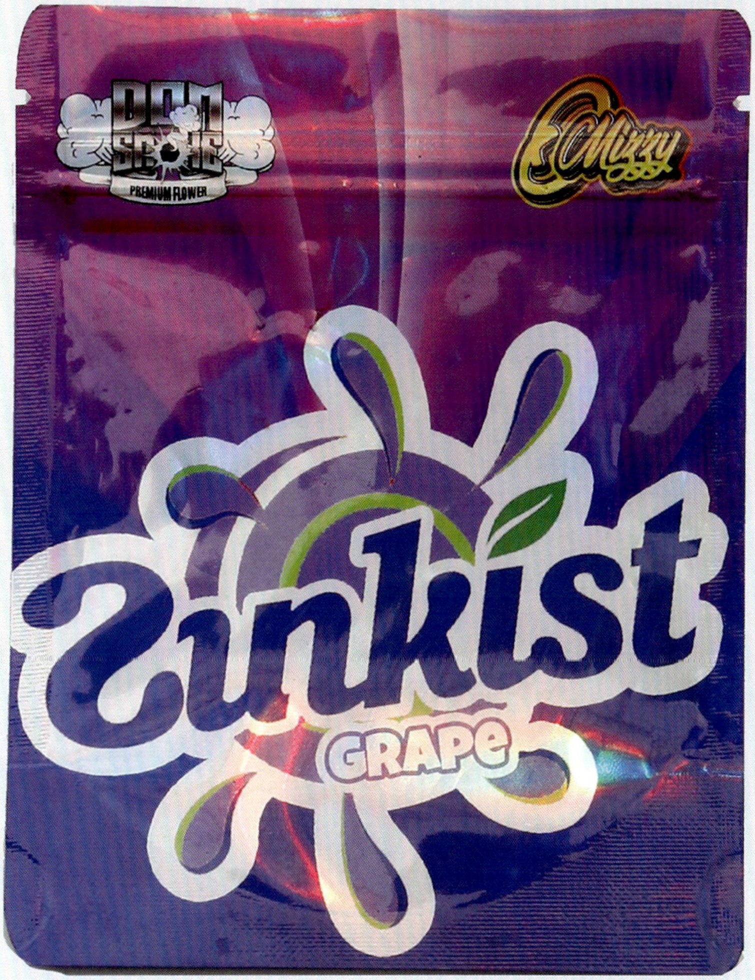
PREMIUM FLOWER
Mizzy
Zinkist
GRAPE

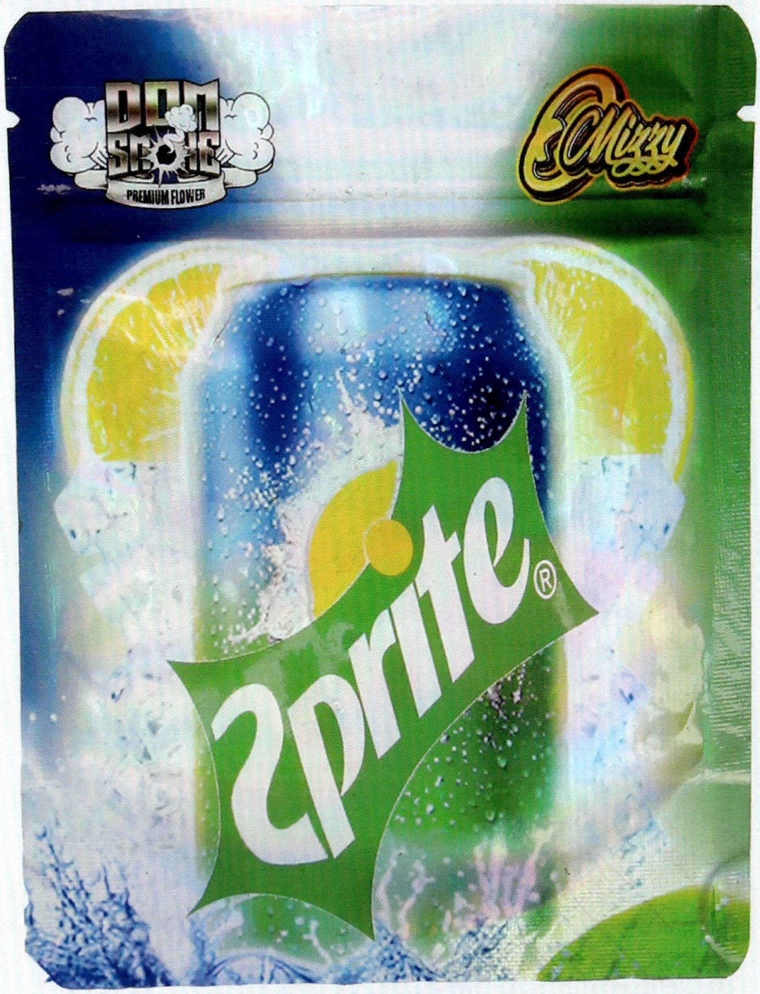
PREMIUM FLOWER
Mizzy
Sprite®

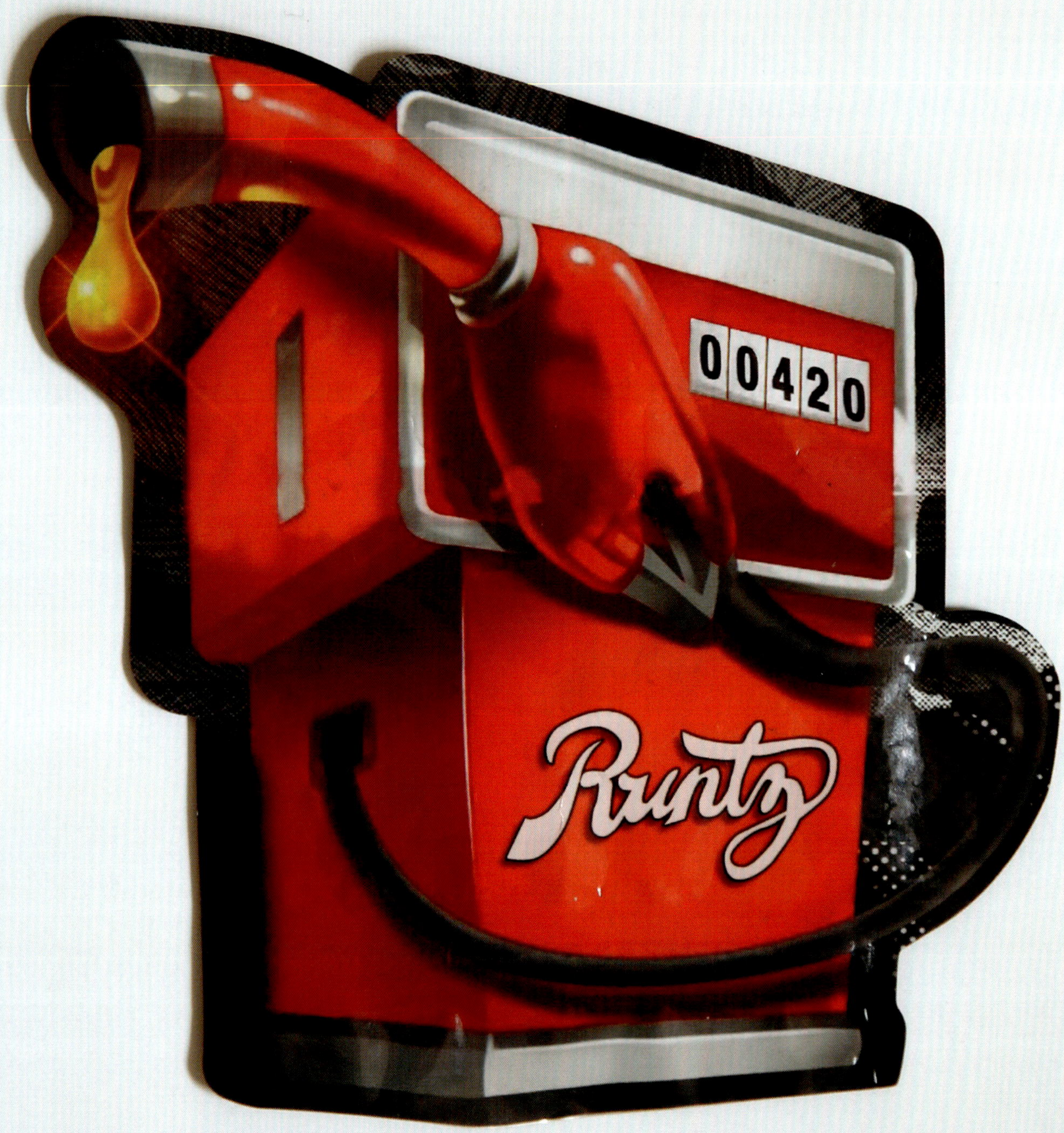

00420
Runtz

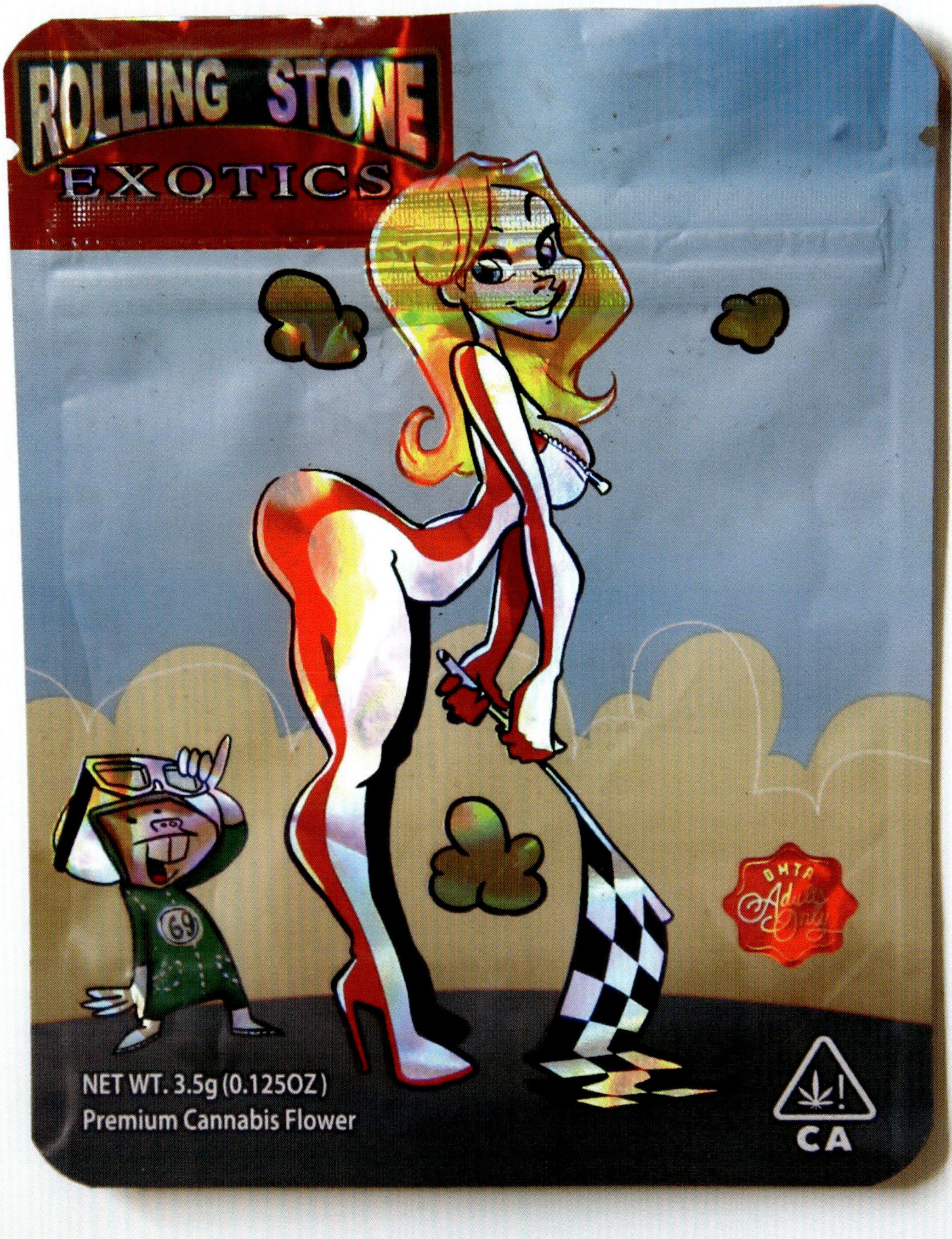
ROLLING STONE
EXOTICS
69
NET WT. 3.5g (0.125OZ)
Premium Cannabis Flower
CA

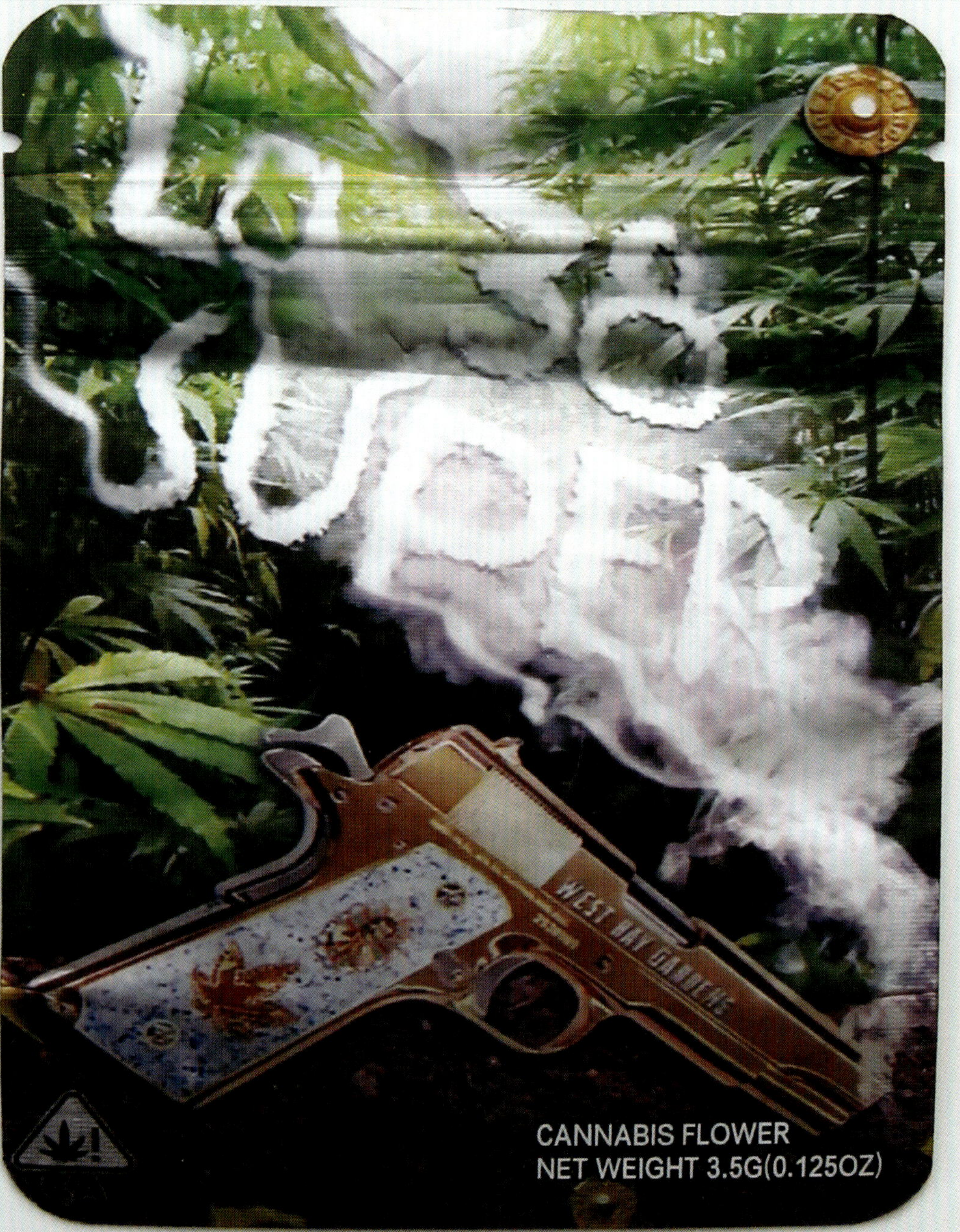
CANNABIS FLOWER
NET WEIGHT 3.5G(0.125OZ)

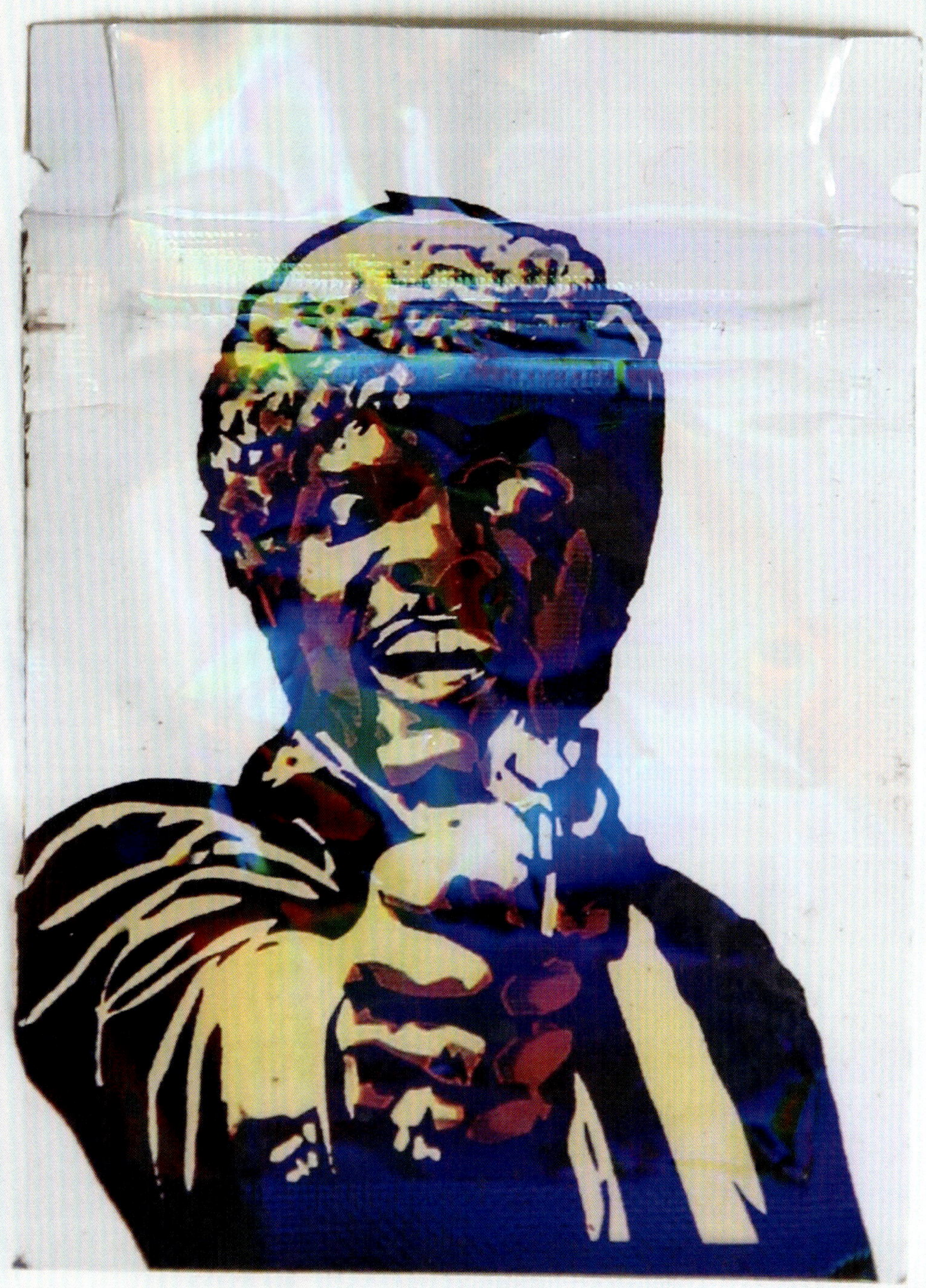

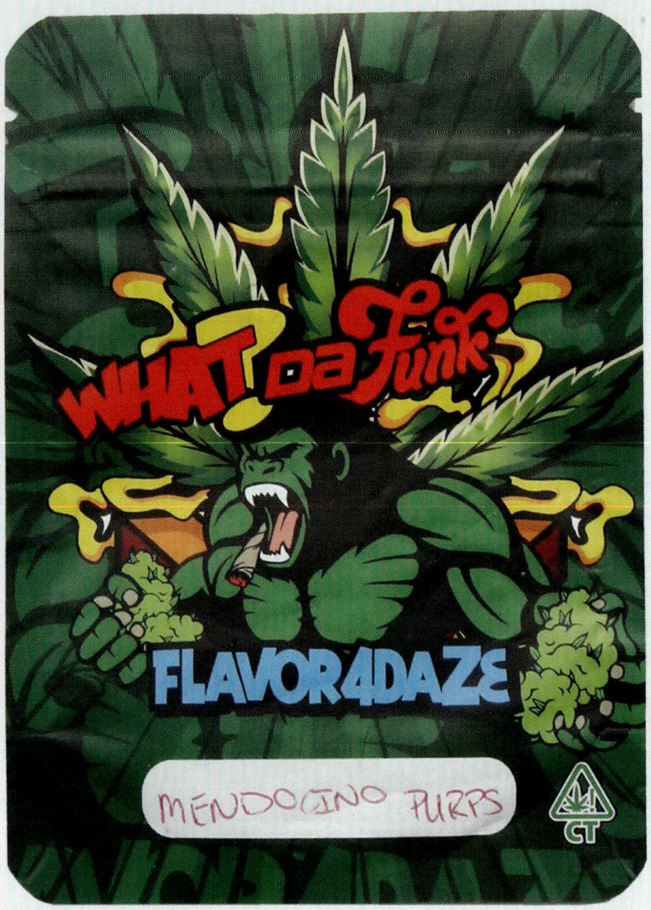
WHAT da Funk
FLAVOR4DAZE
MENDOCINO PURPS
CT

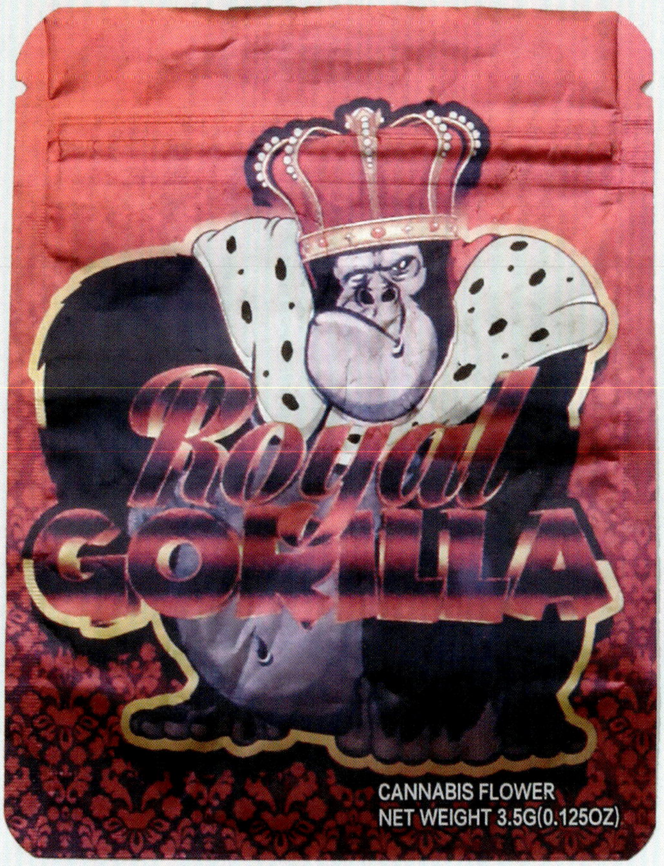
Royal
GORILLA
CANNABIS FLOWER
NET WEIGHT 3.5G(0.125OZ)

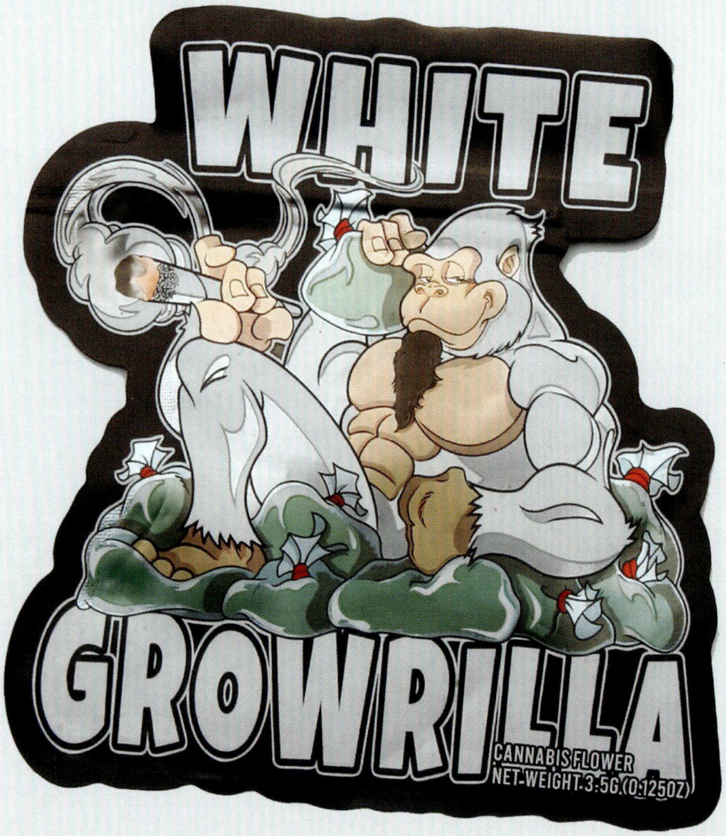
WHITE
GROWRILLA
CANNABIS FLOWER
NET-WEIGHT 3.5G (0.125OZ)

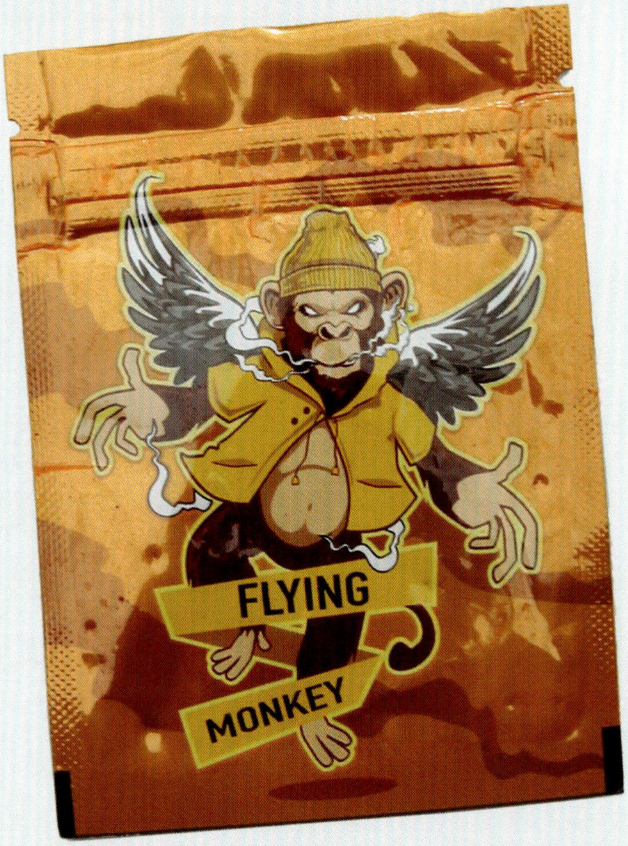
FLYING
MONKEY

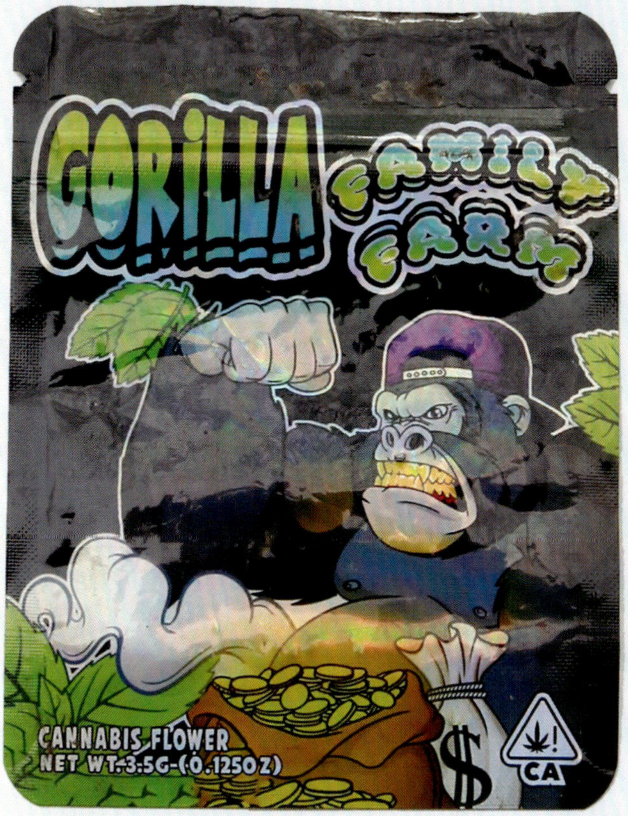
GORILLA
FAMILY FARM
CANNABIS FLOWER
NET WT-3.5G-(0.125OZ)
CA

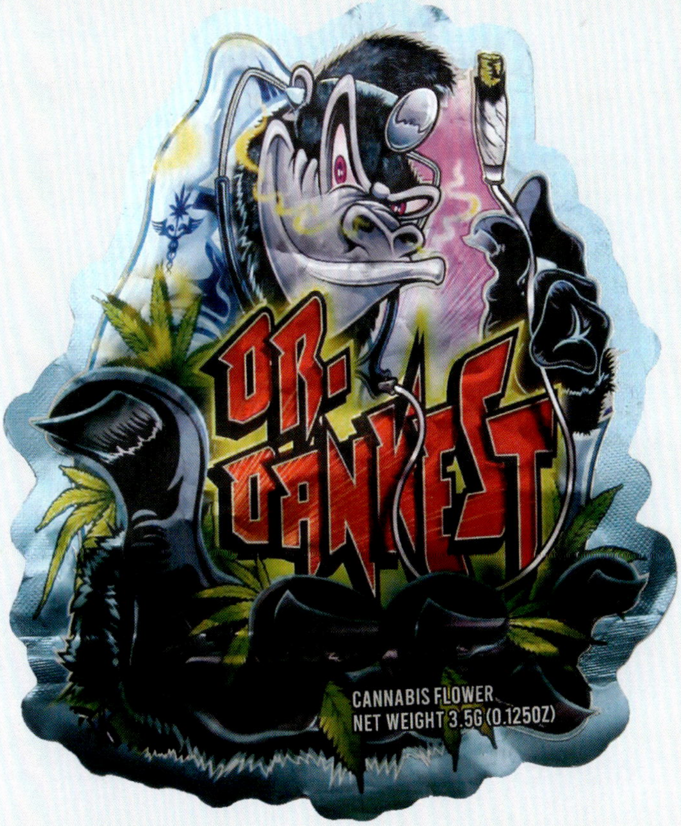
DR. DANKEST
CANNABIS FLOWER
NET WEIGHT 3.5G (0.125OZ)

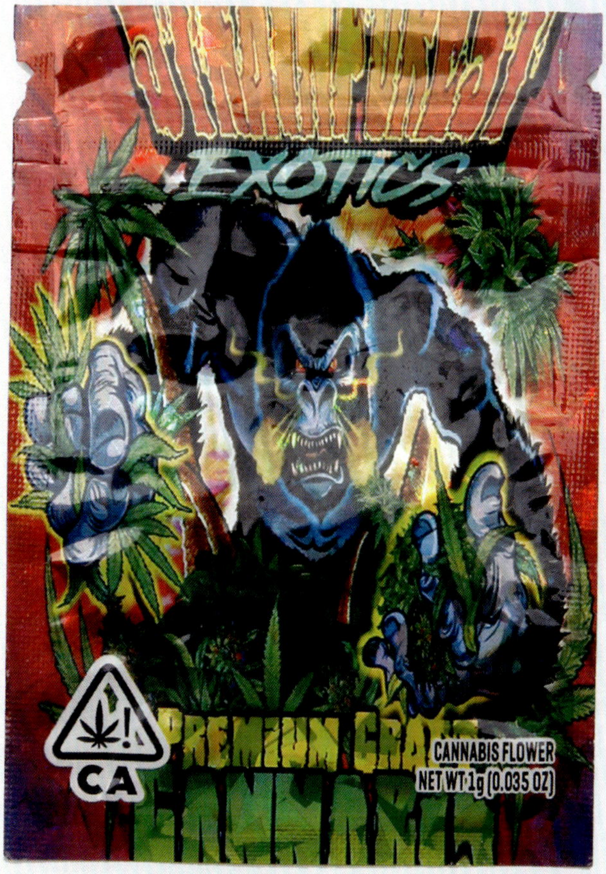
EXOTICS
CA
CANNABIS FLOWER
NET WT 1g (0.035 OZ)

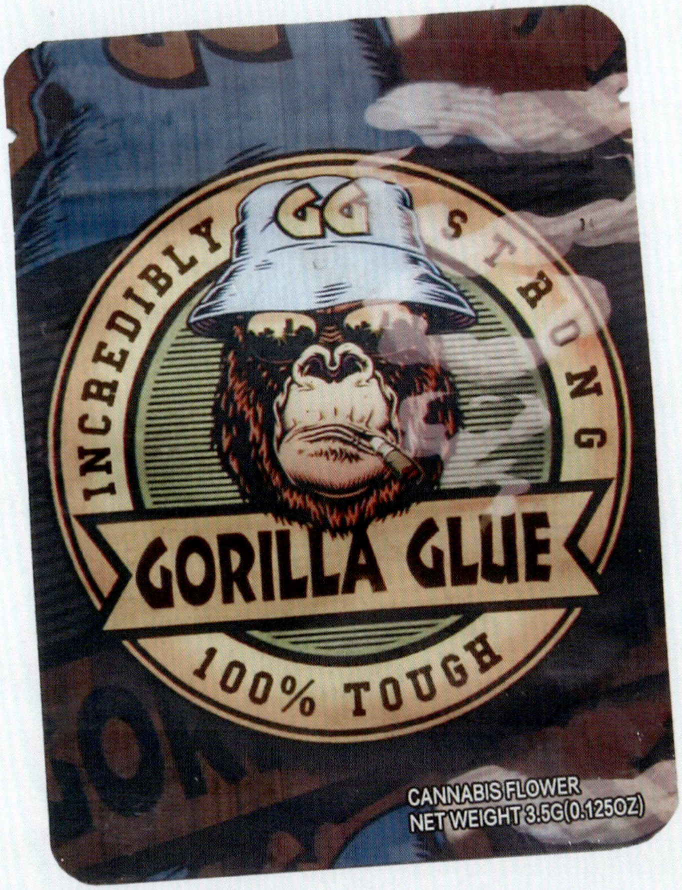
GG
INCREDIBLY STRONG
GORILLA GLUE
100% TOUGH
CANNABIS FLOWER
NET WEIGHT 3.5G (0.125OZ)

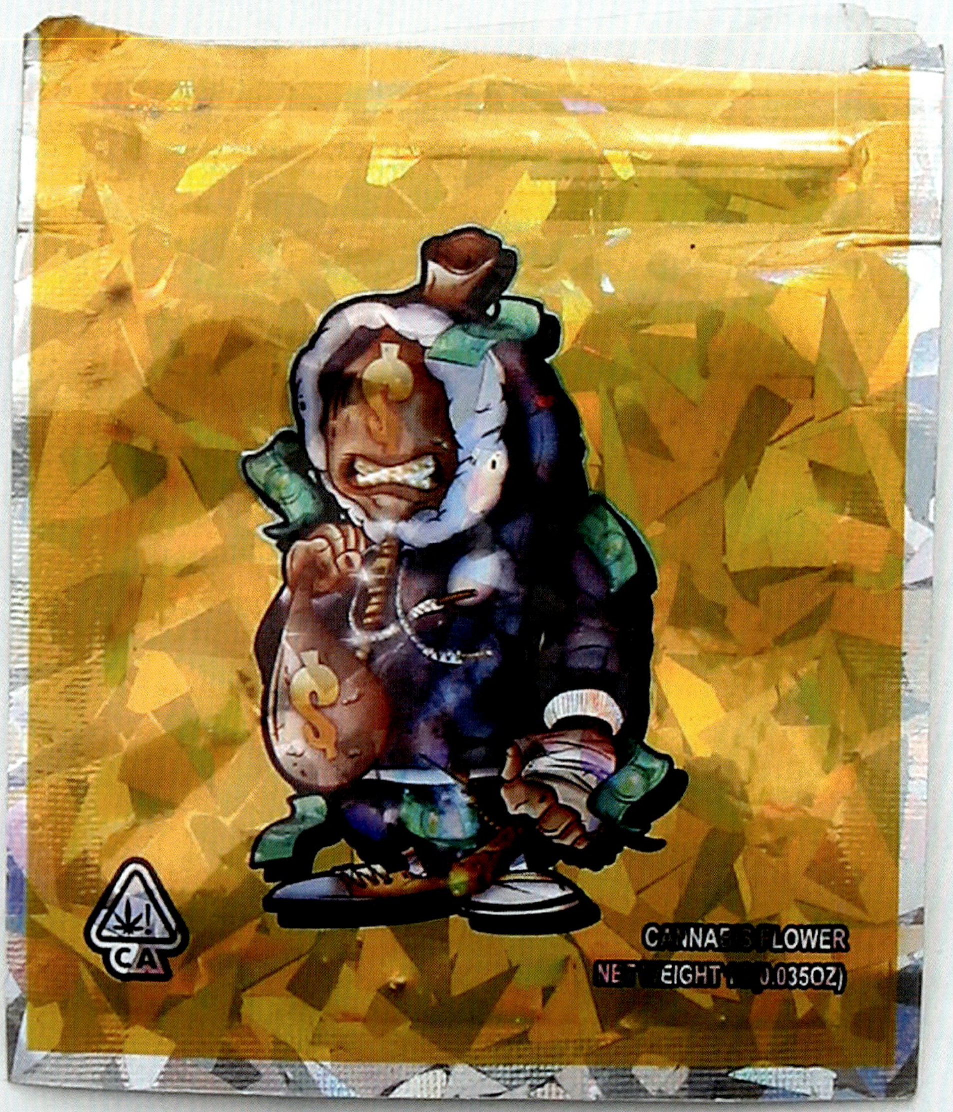
CA
CANNABIS FLOWER

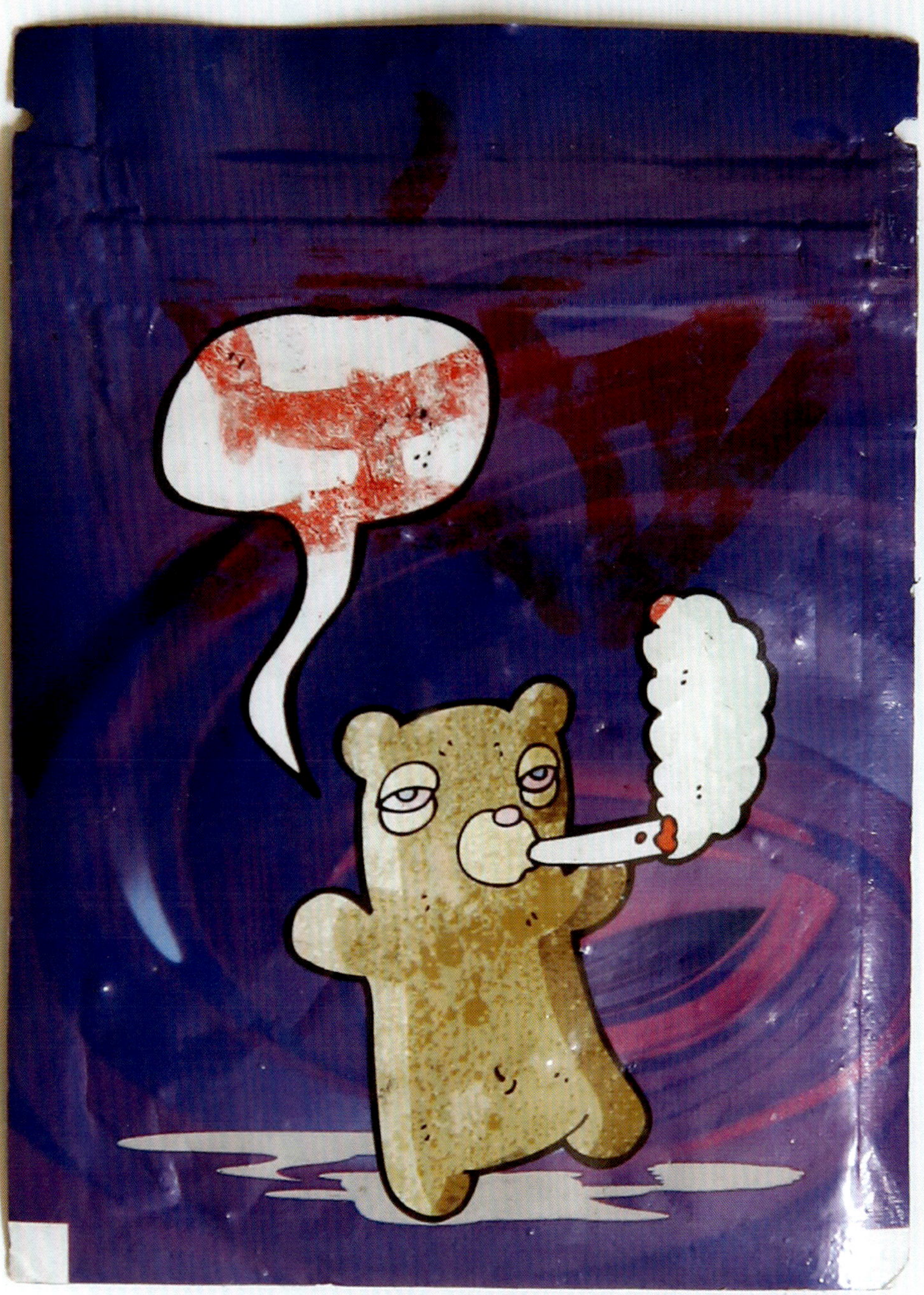

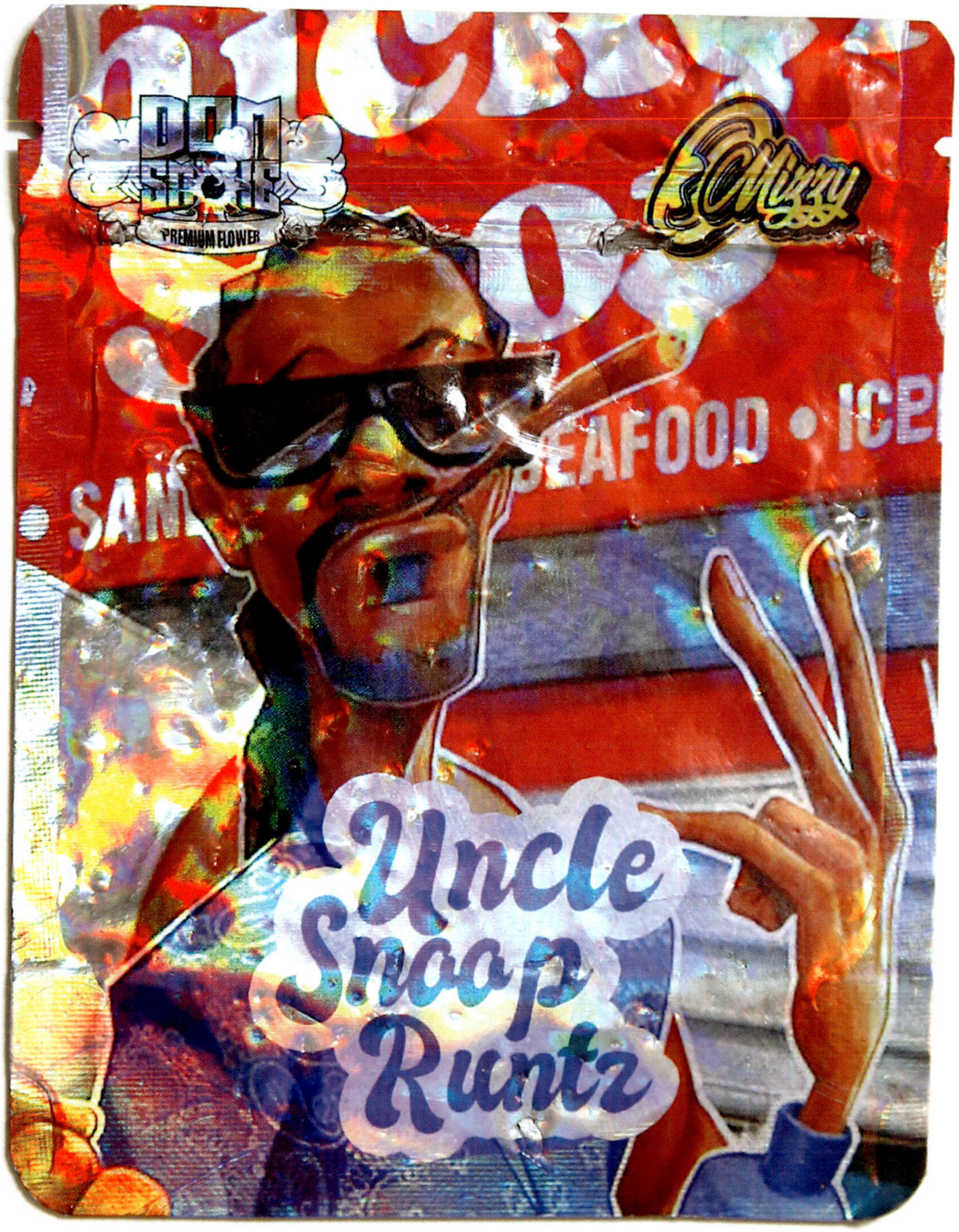
PREMIUM FLOWER
SEAFOOD • ICE
Uncle
Snoop
Runtz

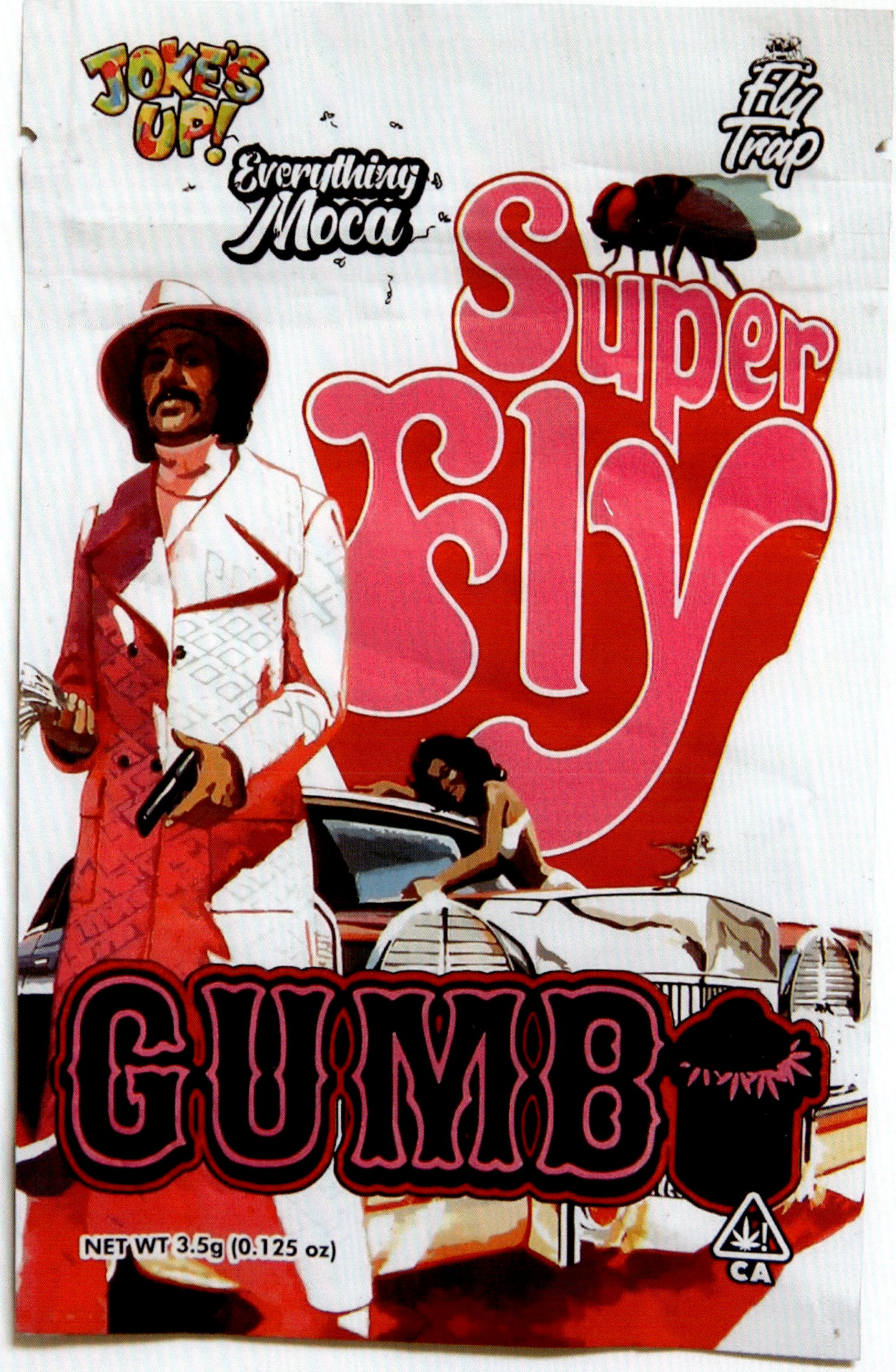
JOKE'S UP!
Everything Moca
Fly Trap
Super Fly
GUMBO
NET WT 3.5g (0.125 oz)
CA

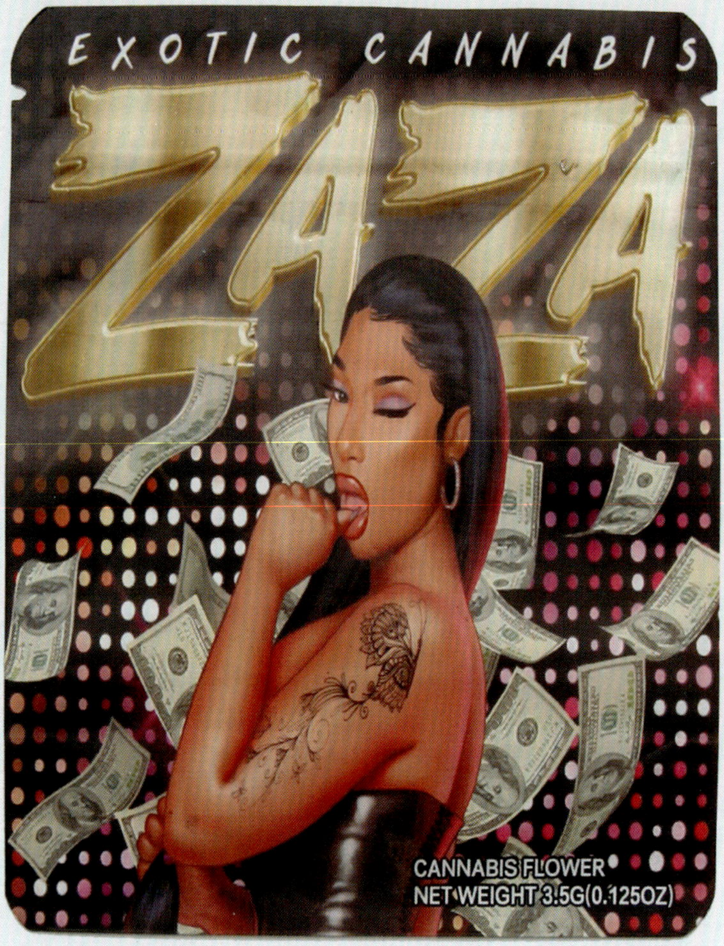
EXOTIC CANNABIS
ZAZA
CANNABIS FLOWER
NET WEIGHT 3.5G(0.125OZ)

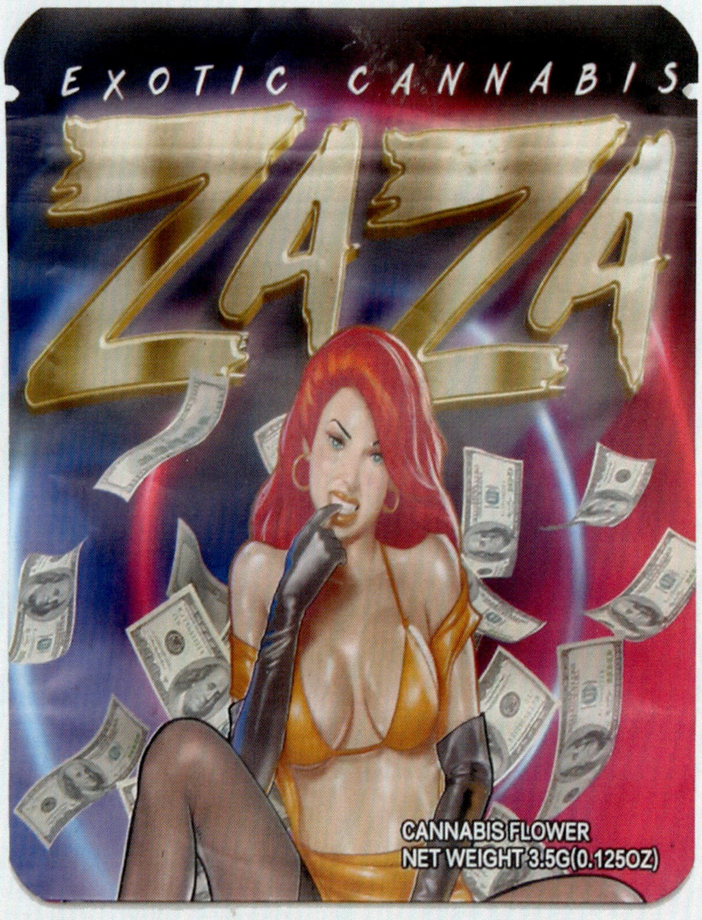
EXOTIC CANNABIS
ZAZA
CANNABIS FLOWER
NET WEIGHT 3.5G(0.125OZ)

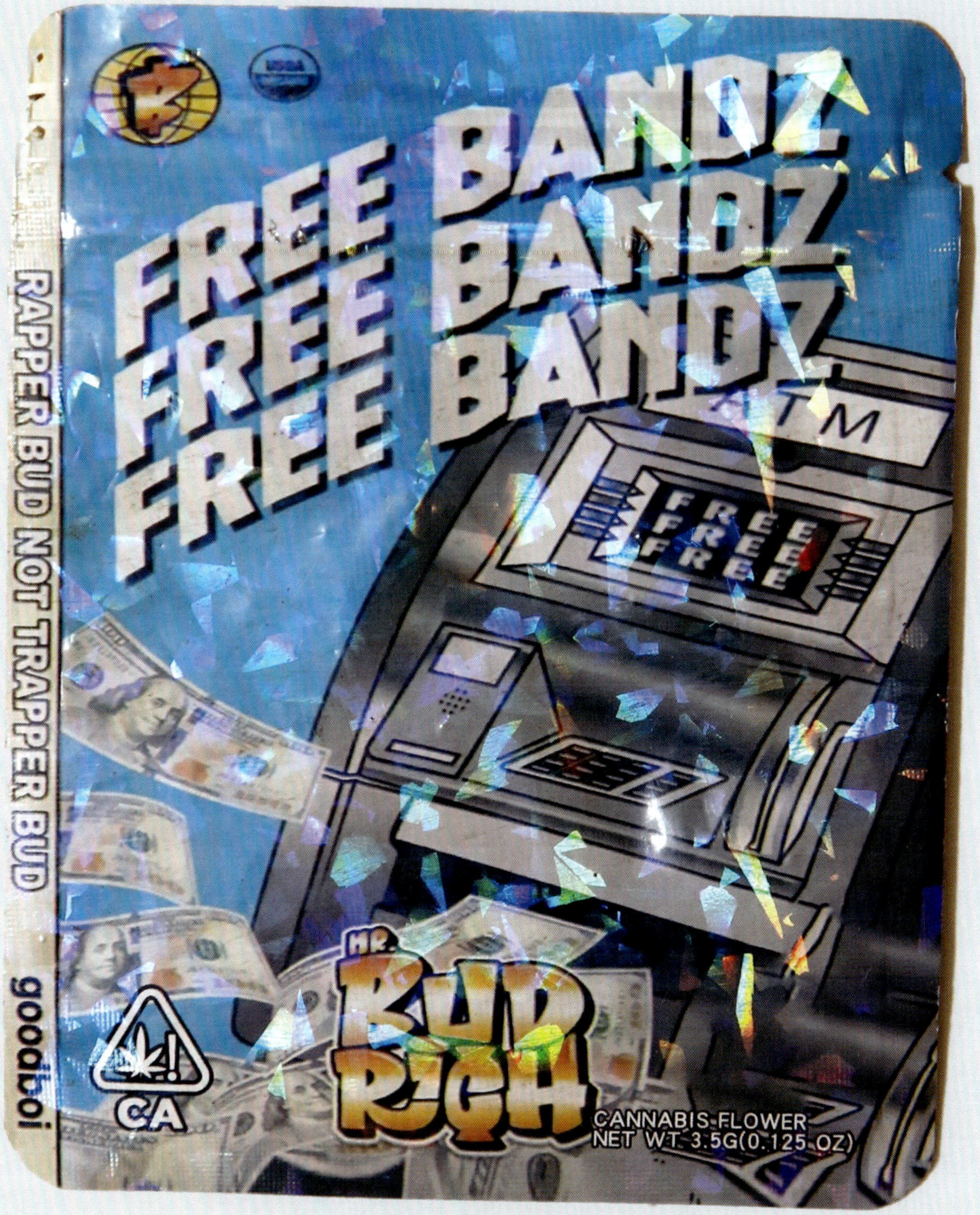
FREE BANDZ
FREE BANDZ
FREE BANDZ
ATM
FREE
FREE
FREE
RAPPER BUD NOT TRAPPER BUD
goodboi
CA
MR. BUD RICH
CANNABIS FLOWER
NET WT 3.5G(0.125 OZ)

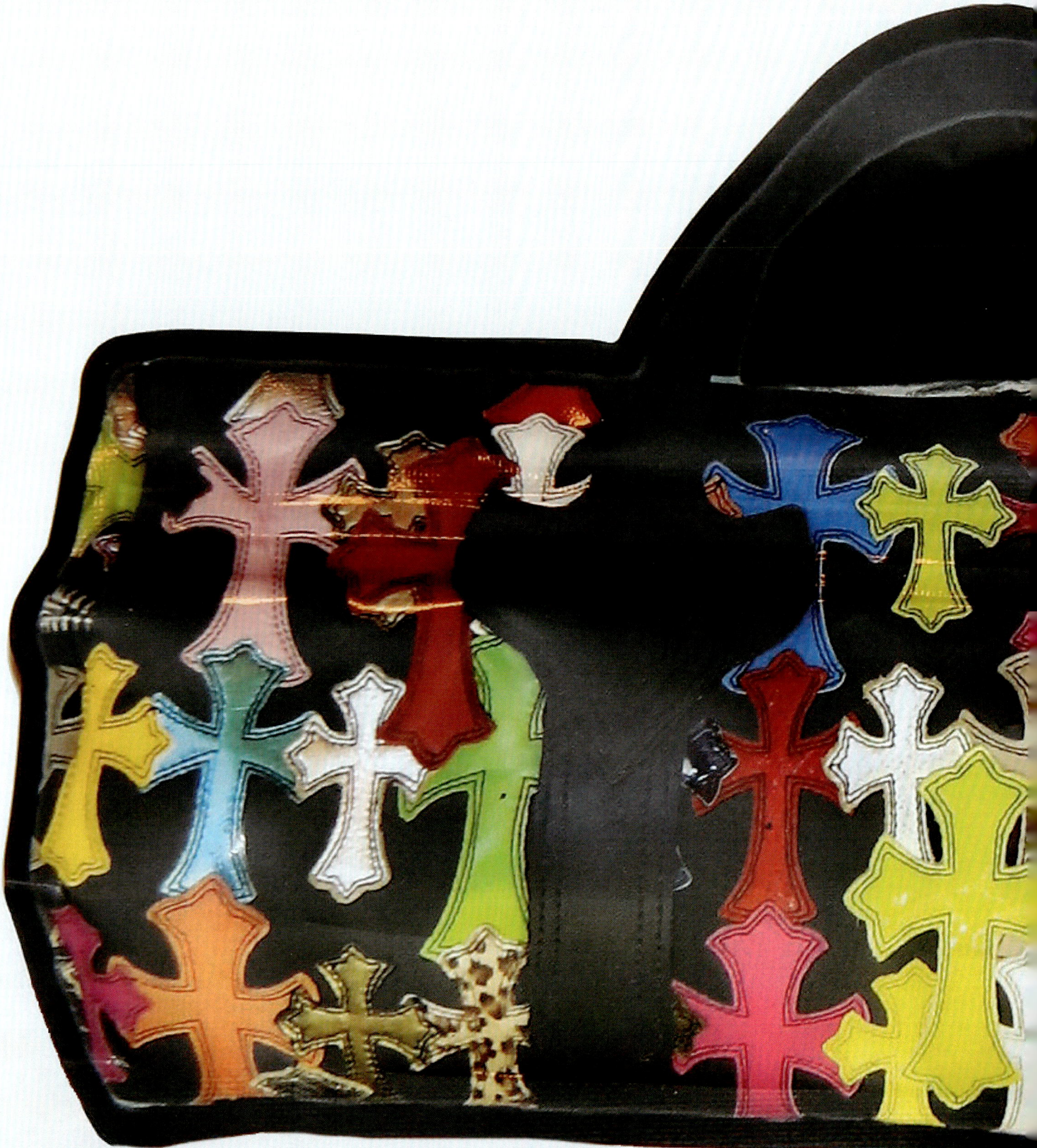

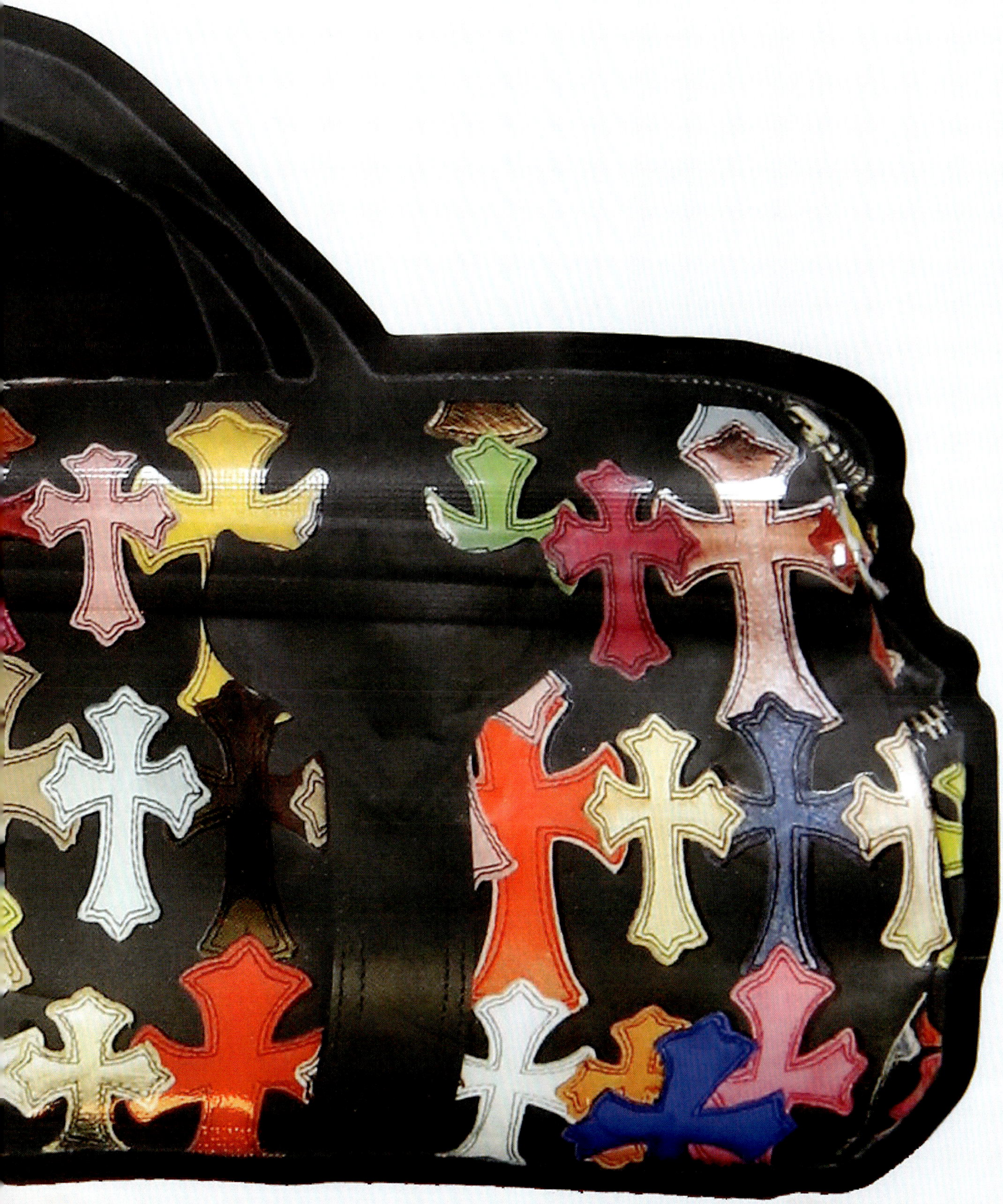

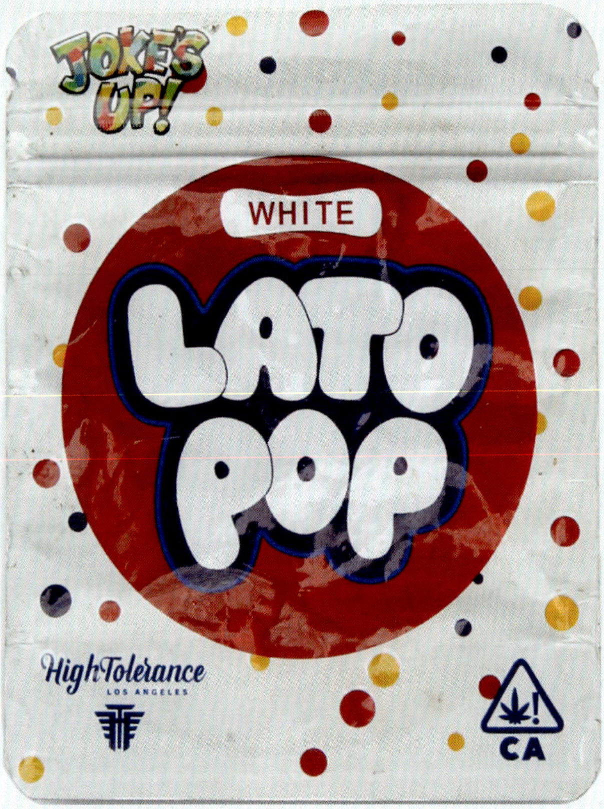
JOKE'S UP!
WHITE
LATO POP
HighTolerance
LOS ANGELES
CA

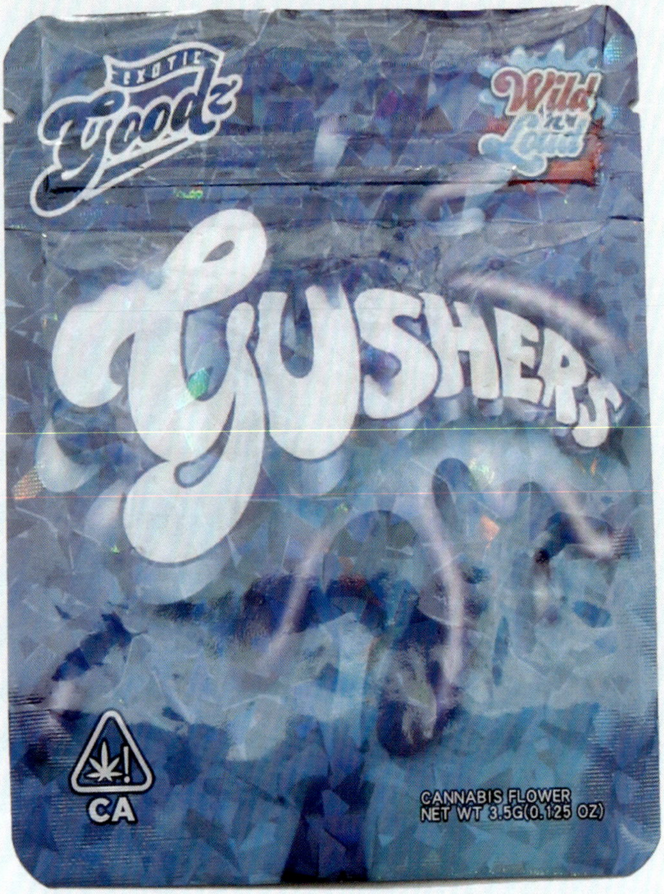
Gushers
CA
CANNABIS FLOWER
NET WT 3.5G(0.125 OZ)

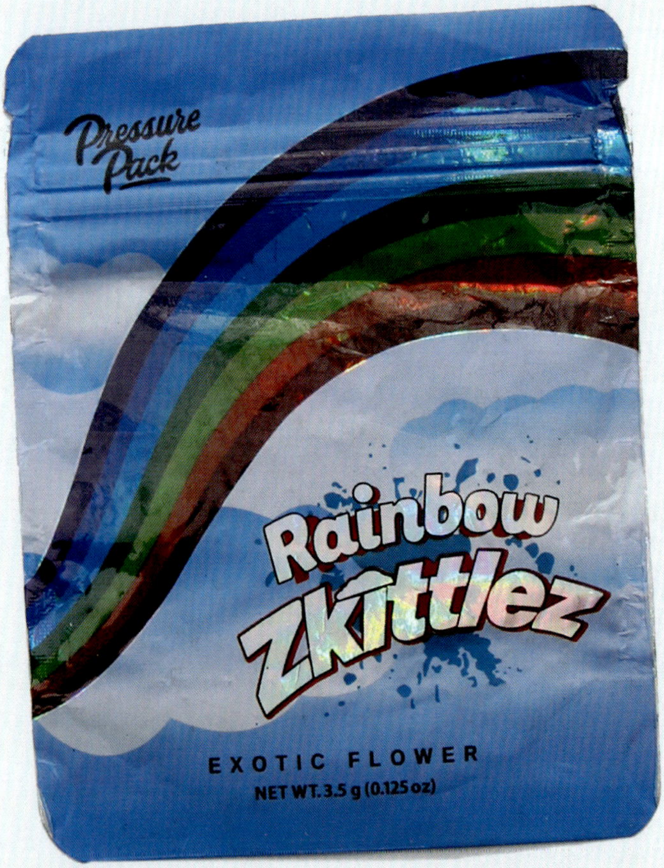
Pressure Pack
Rainbow
Zkittlez
EXOTIC FLOWER
NET WT. 3.5 g (0.125 oz)

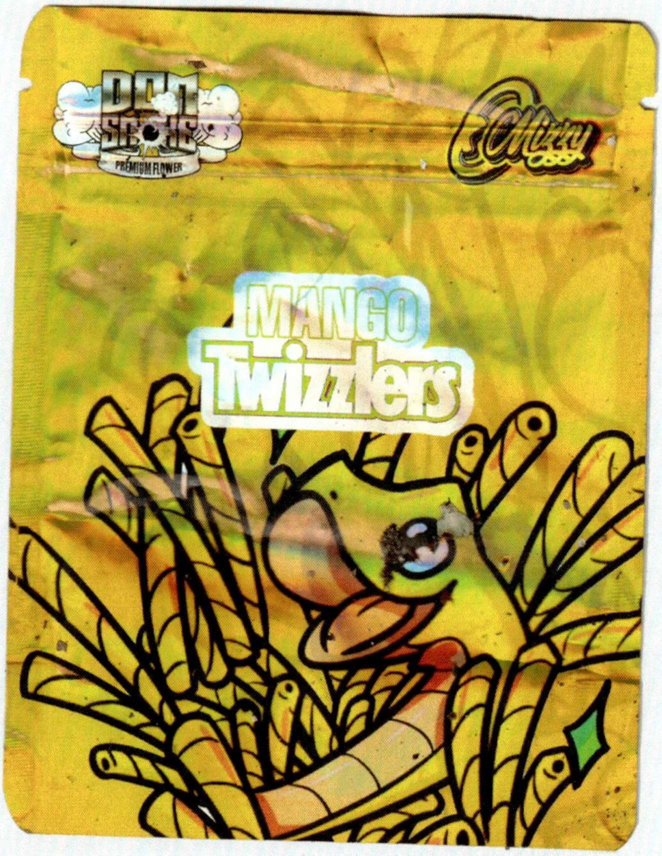
PREMIUM FLOWER
MANGO
Twizzlers

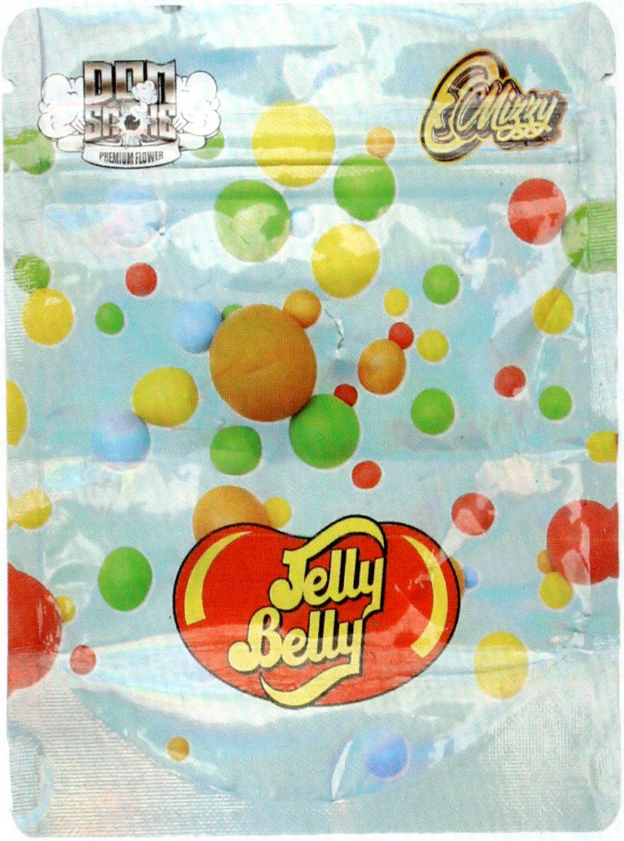
PREMIUM FLOWER
Jelly
Belly

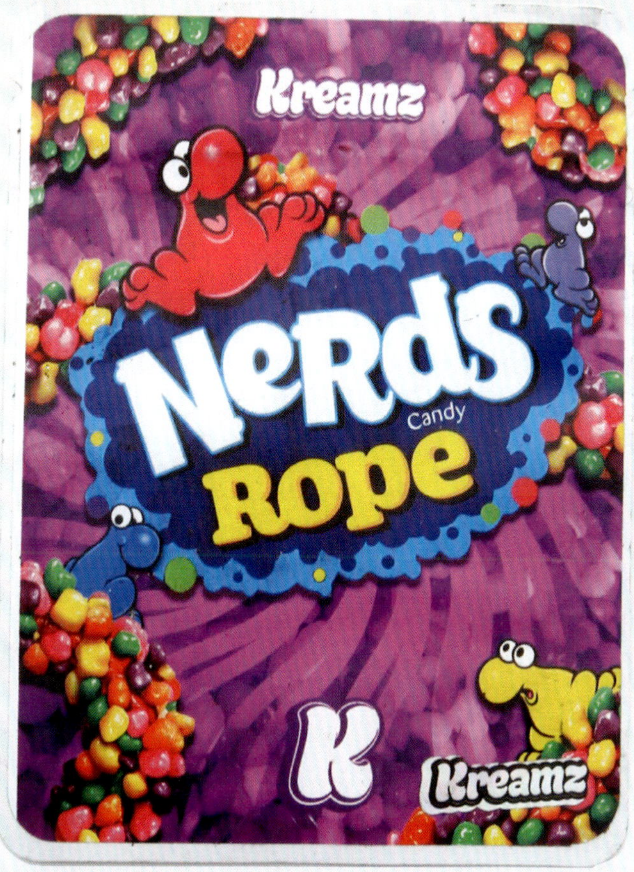
Kreamz
Nerds
Candy
Rope
K
Kreamz

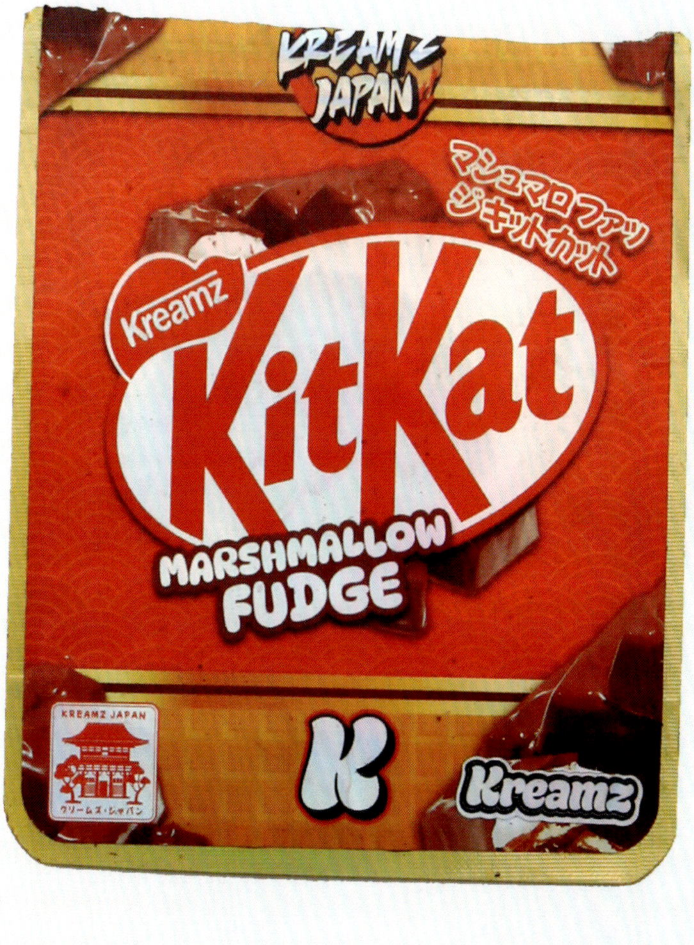
KREAMZ
JAPAN
マシュマロファッ
ジキットカット
Kreamz
KitKat
MARSHMALLOW
FUDGE
KREAMZ JAPAN
クリームズ・ジャパン
K
Kreamz

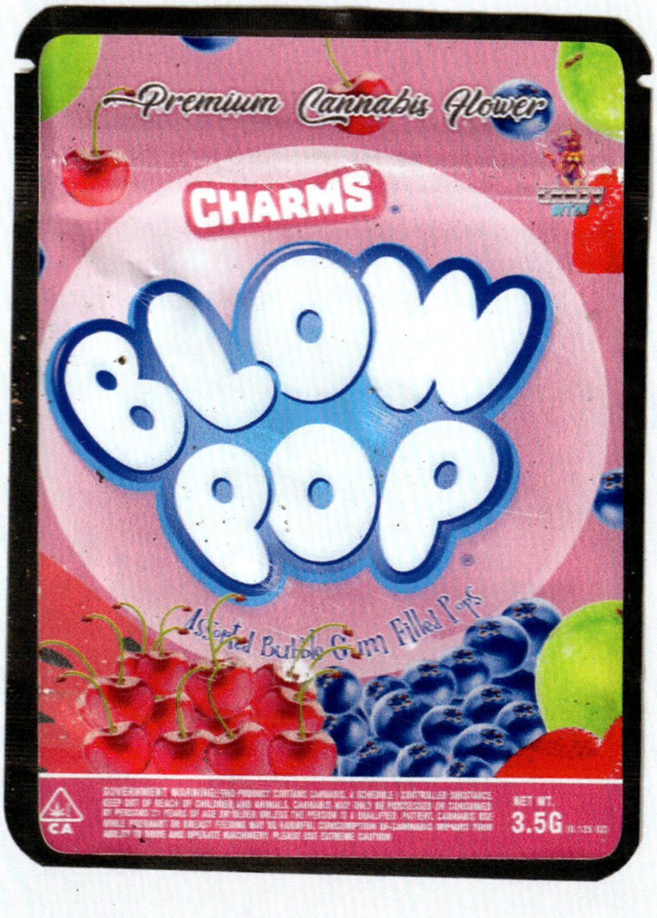
Premium Cannabis Flower
CHARMS
BLOW
POP
Assorted Bubble Gum Filled Pops
NET WT.
3.5G

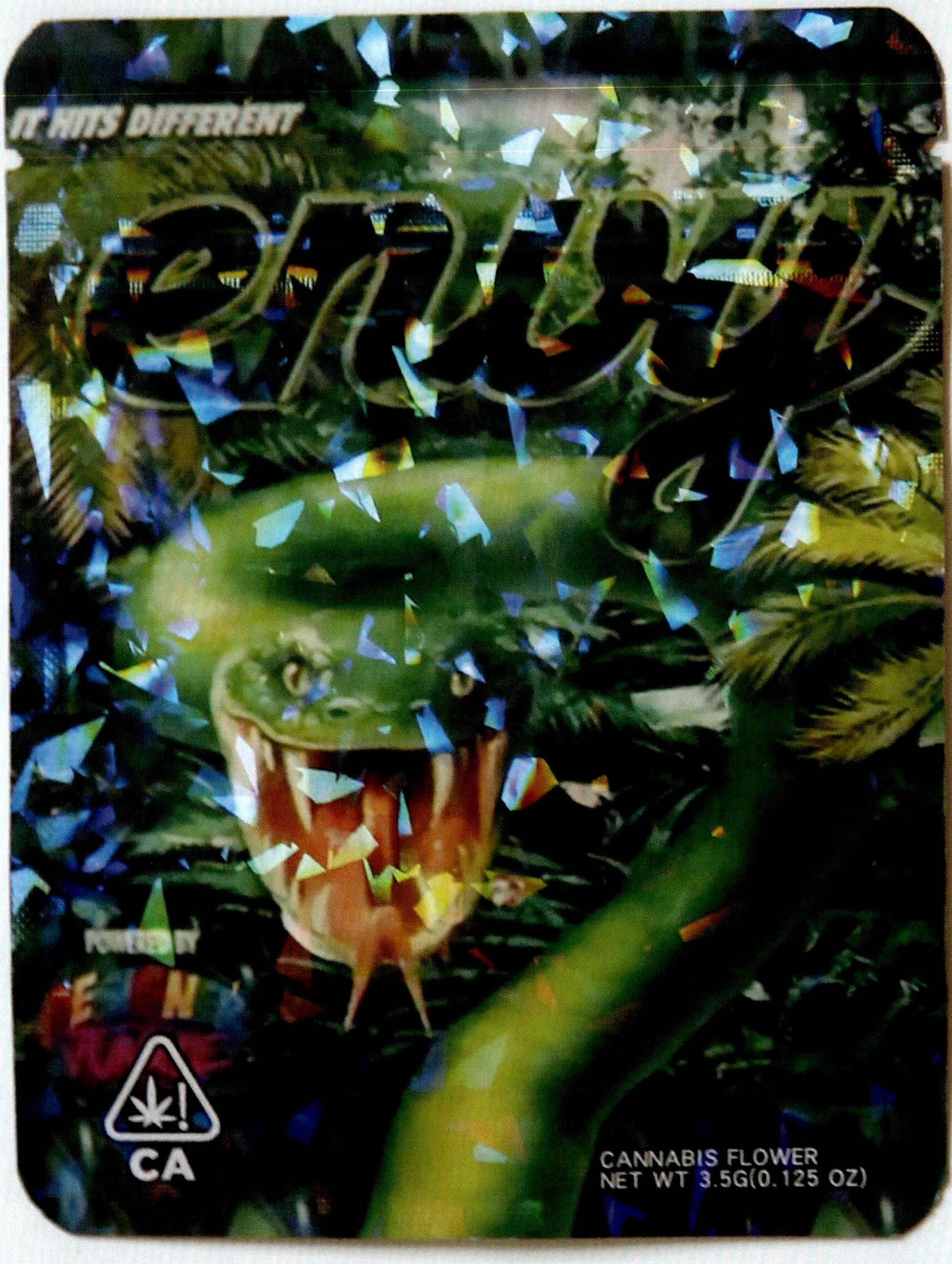
IT HITS DIFFERENT
POWERED BY
CA
CANNABIS FLOWER
NET WT 3.5G(0.125 OZ)

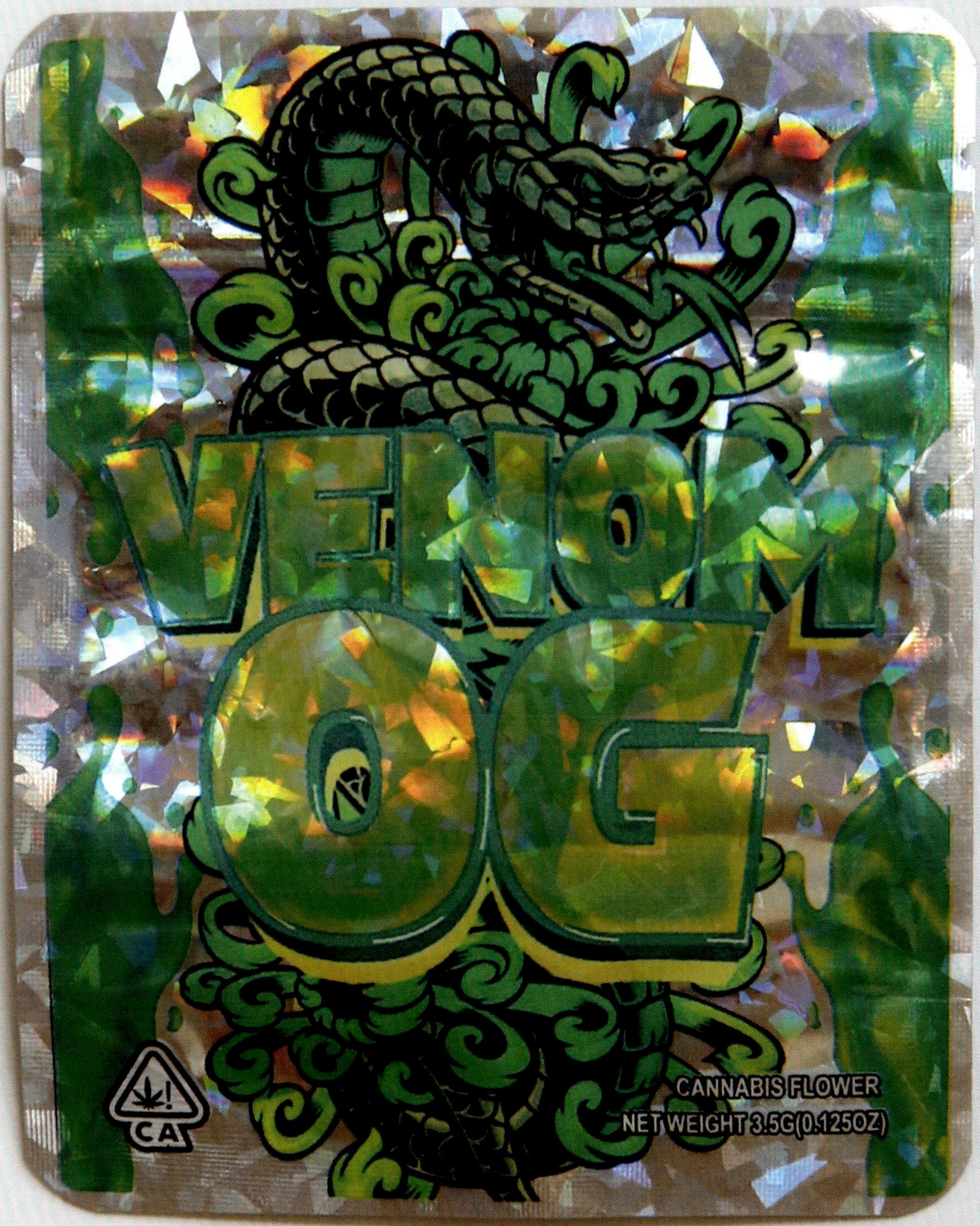

VENOM
OG
CA
CANNABIS FLOWER
NET WEIGHT 3.5G(0.125OZ)

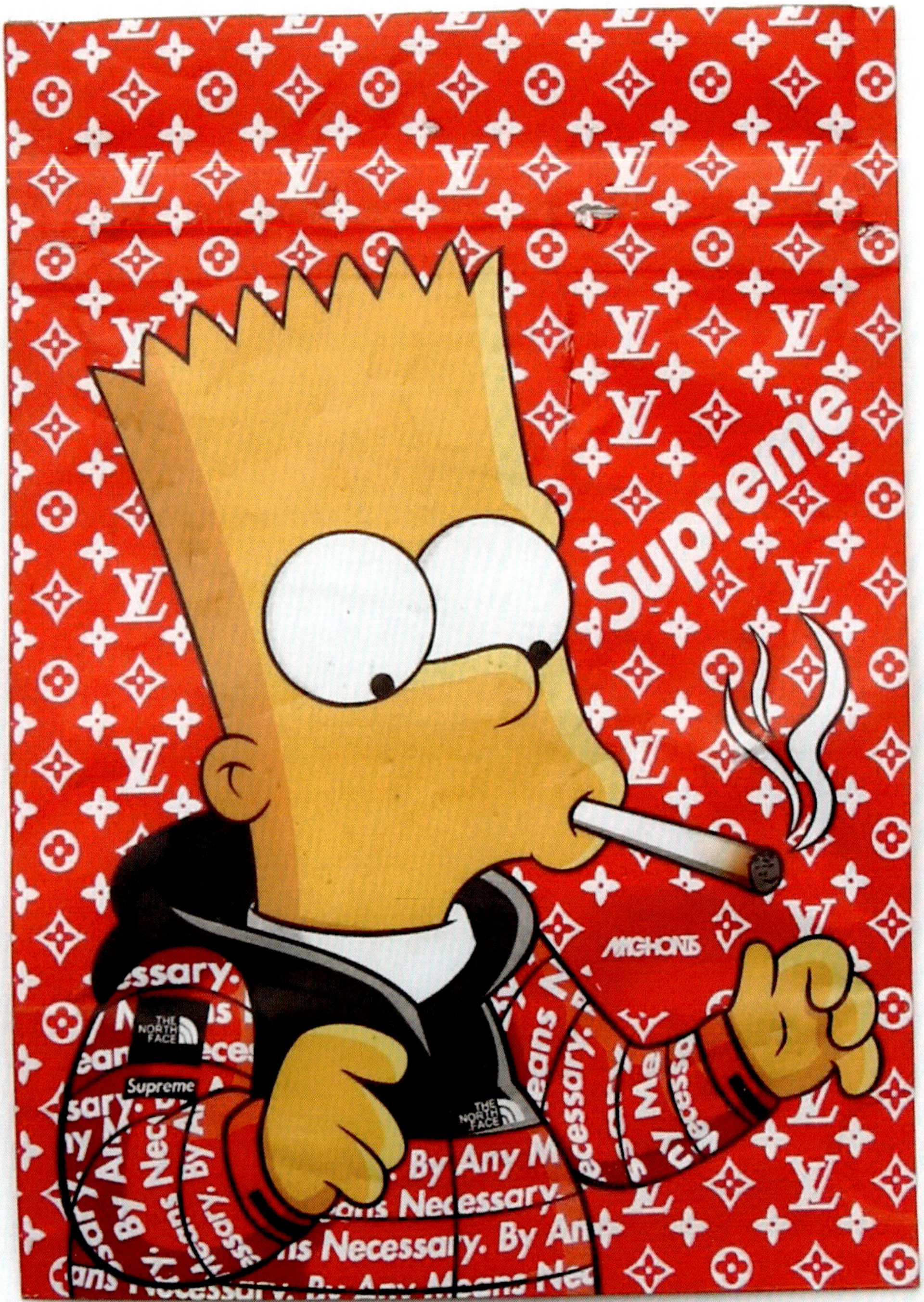
Supreme
THE NORTH FACE
By Any Means Necessary.

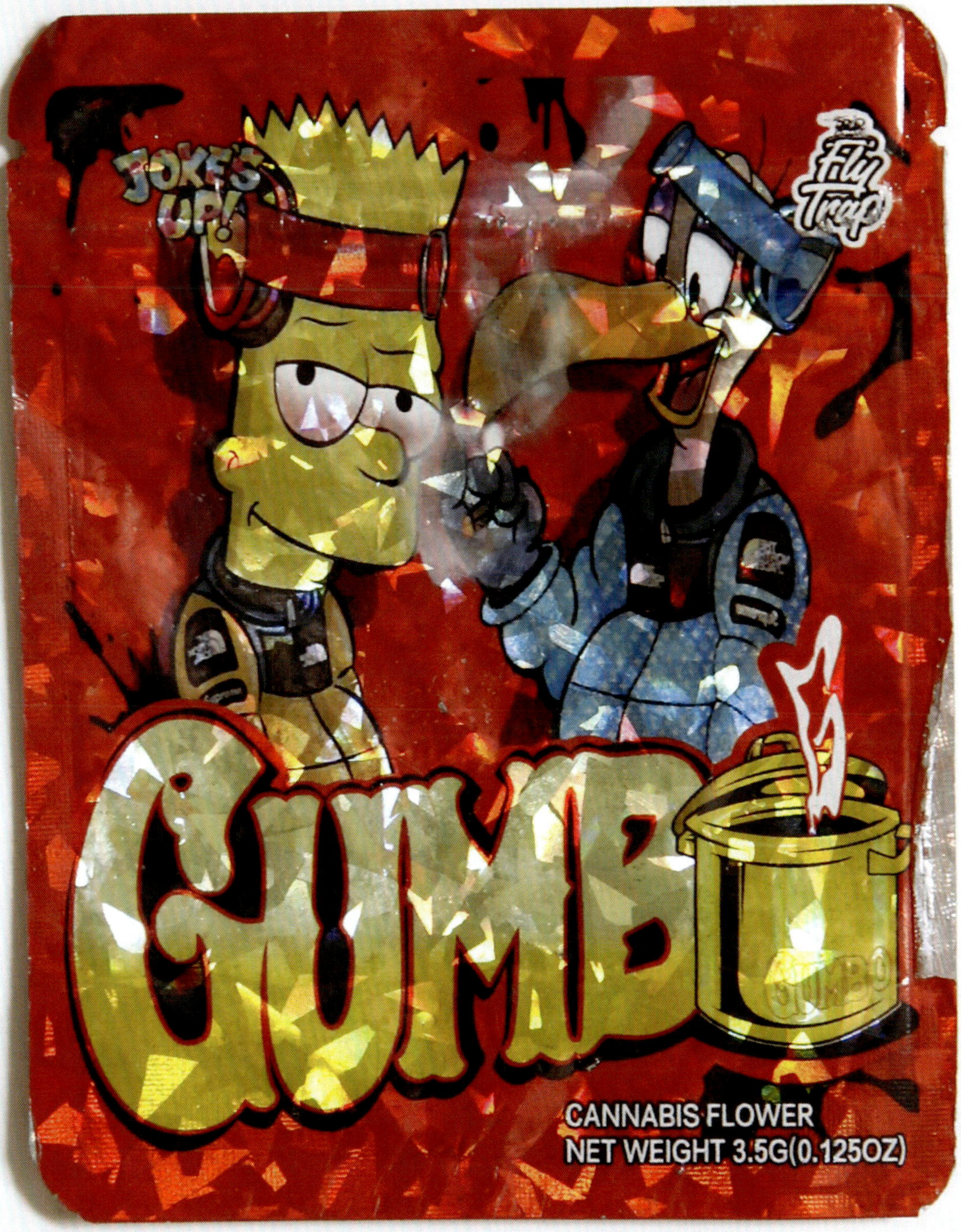
JOKE'S UP!
Fly Trap
GUMBO
CANNABIS FLOWER
NET WEIGHT 3.5G(0.125OZ)

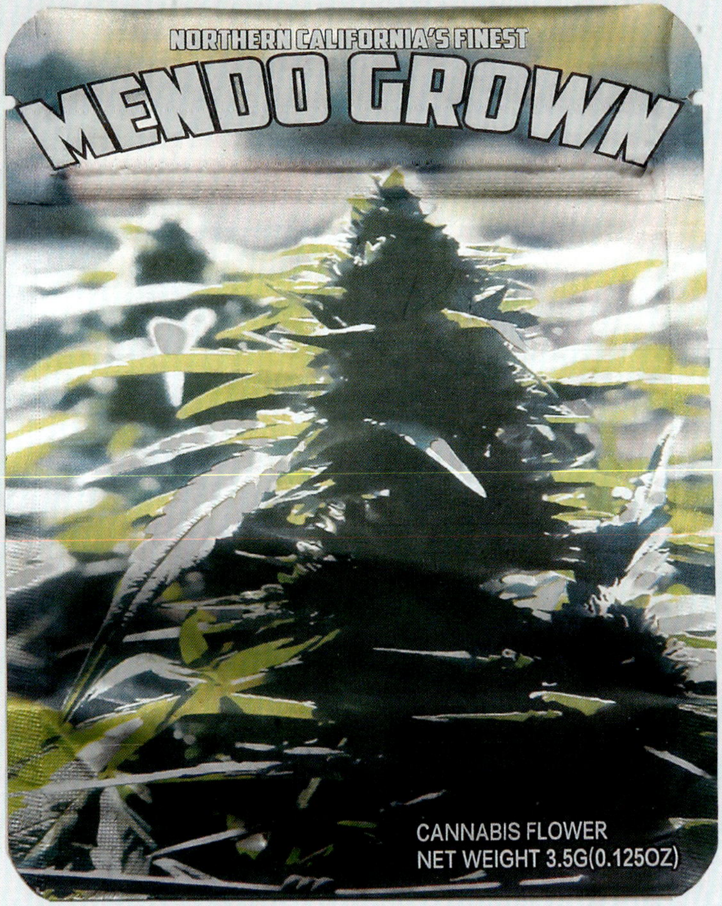
NORTHERN CALIFORNIA'S FINEST
MENDO GROWN
CANNABIS FLOWER
NET WEIGHT 3.5G(0.125OZ)

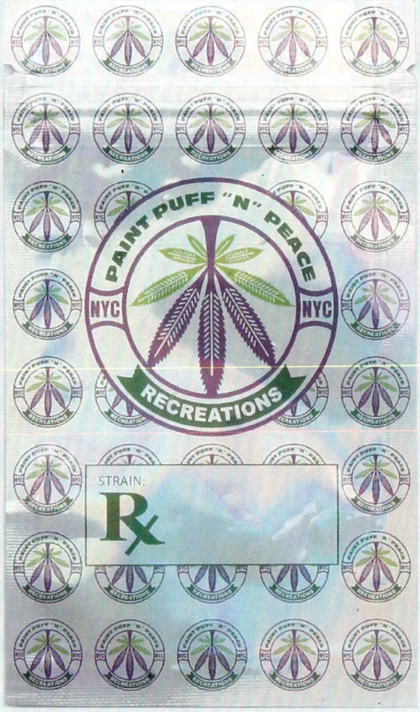
PAINT PUFF "N" PEACE
NYC
NYC
RECREATIONS
STRAIN:
Rx

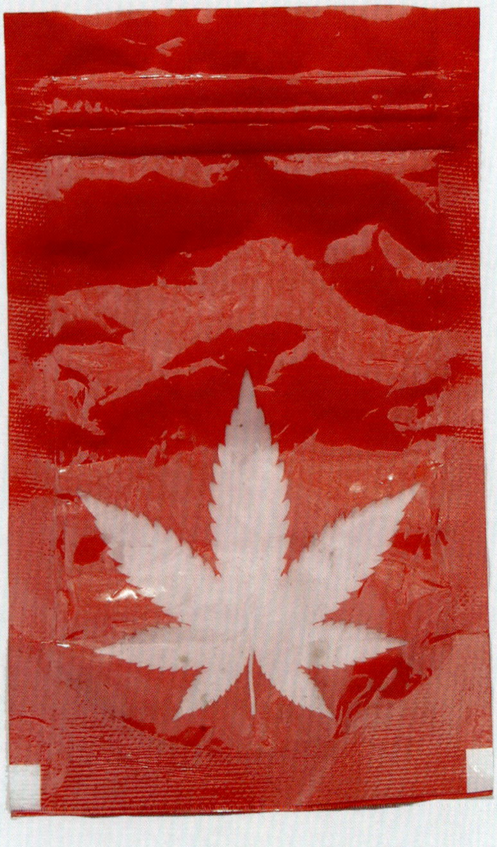

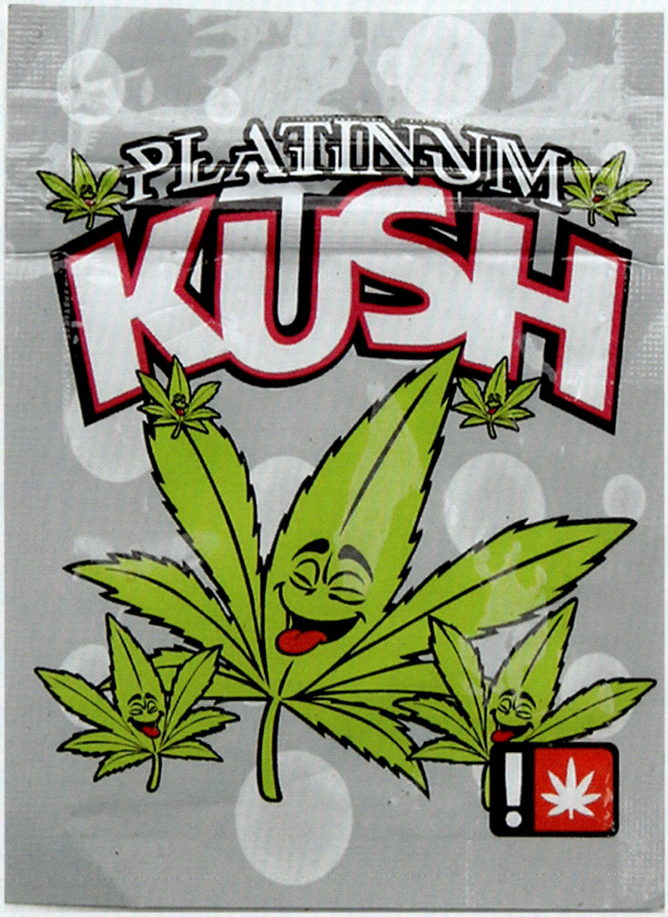
PLATINUM
KUSH

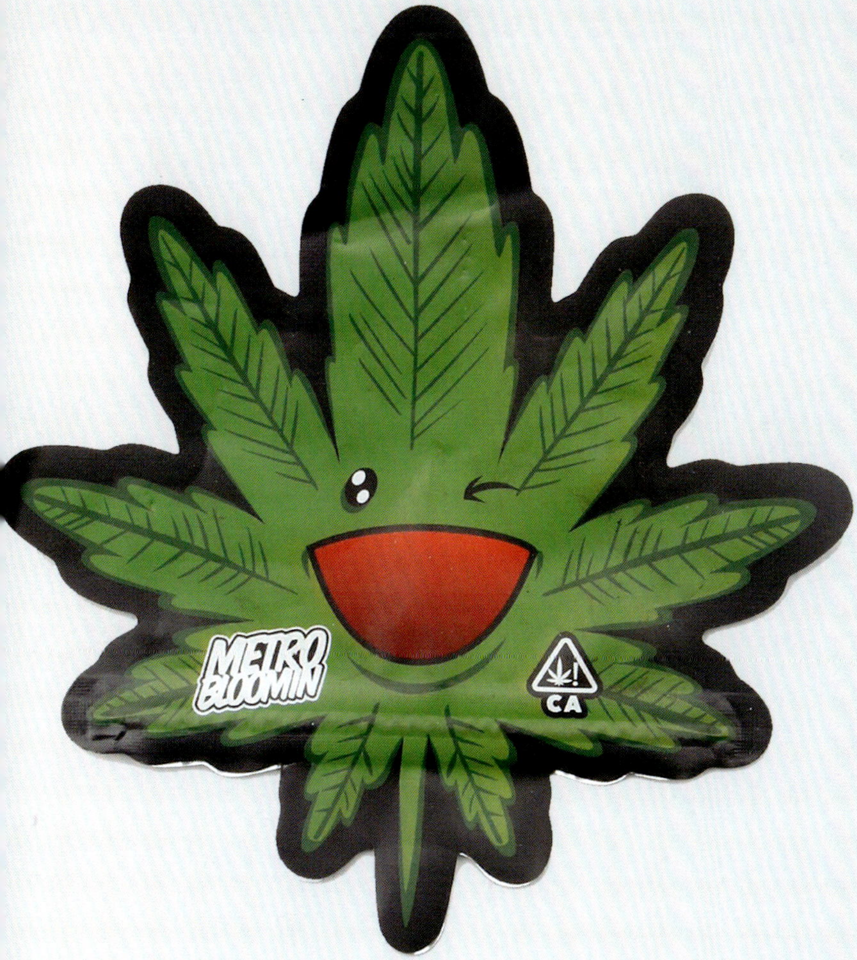
METRO BLOOMIN
CA

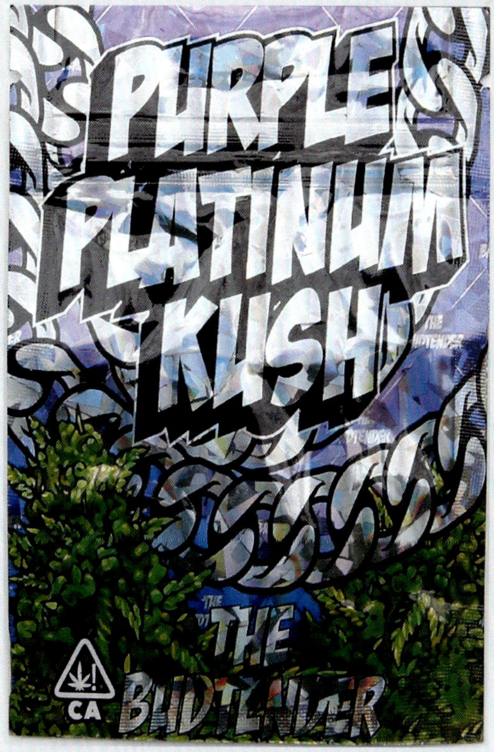
PURPLE PLATINUM KUSH
THE BUDTENDER
CA

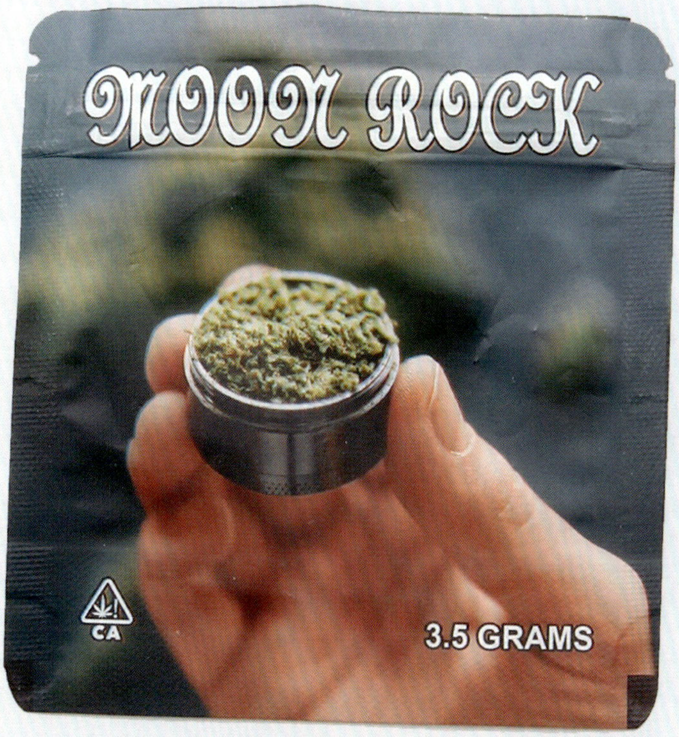
MOON ROCK
CA
3.5 GRAMS

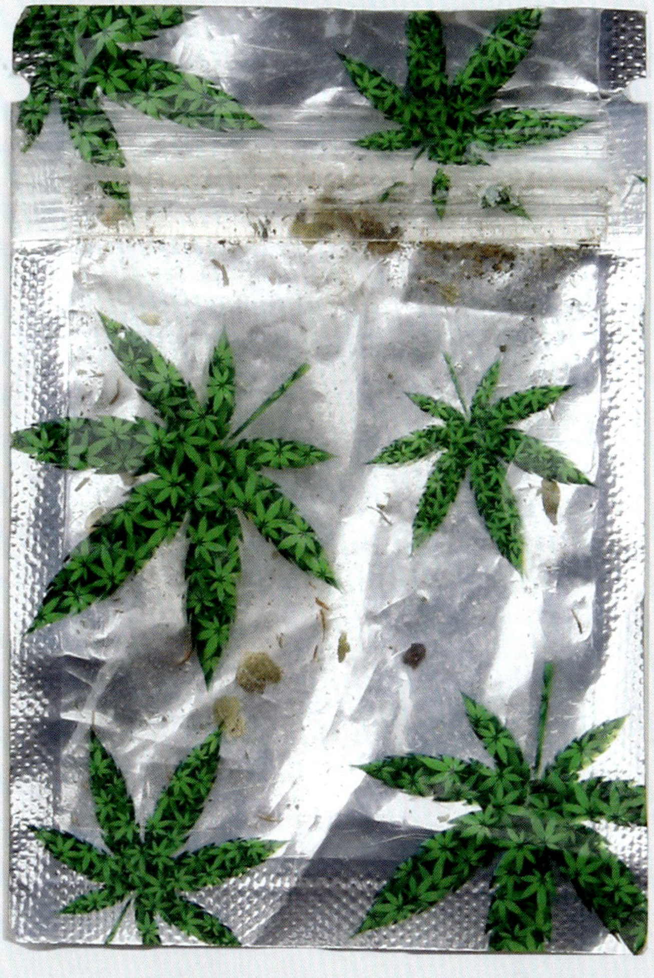

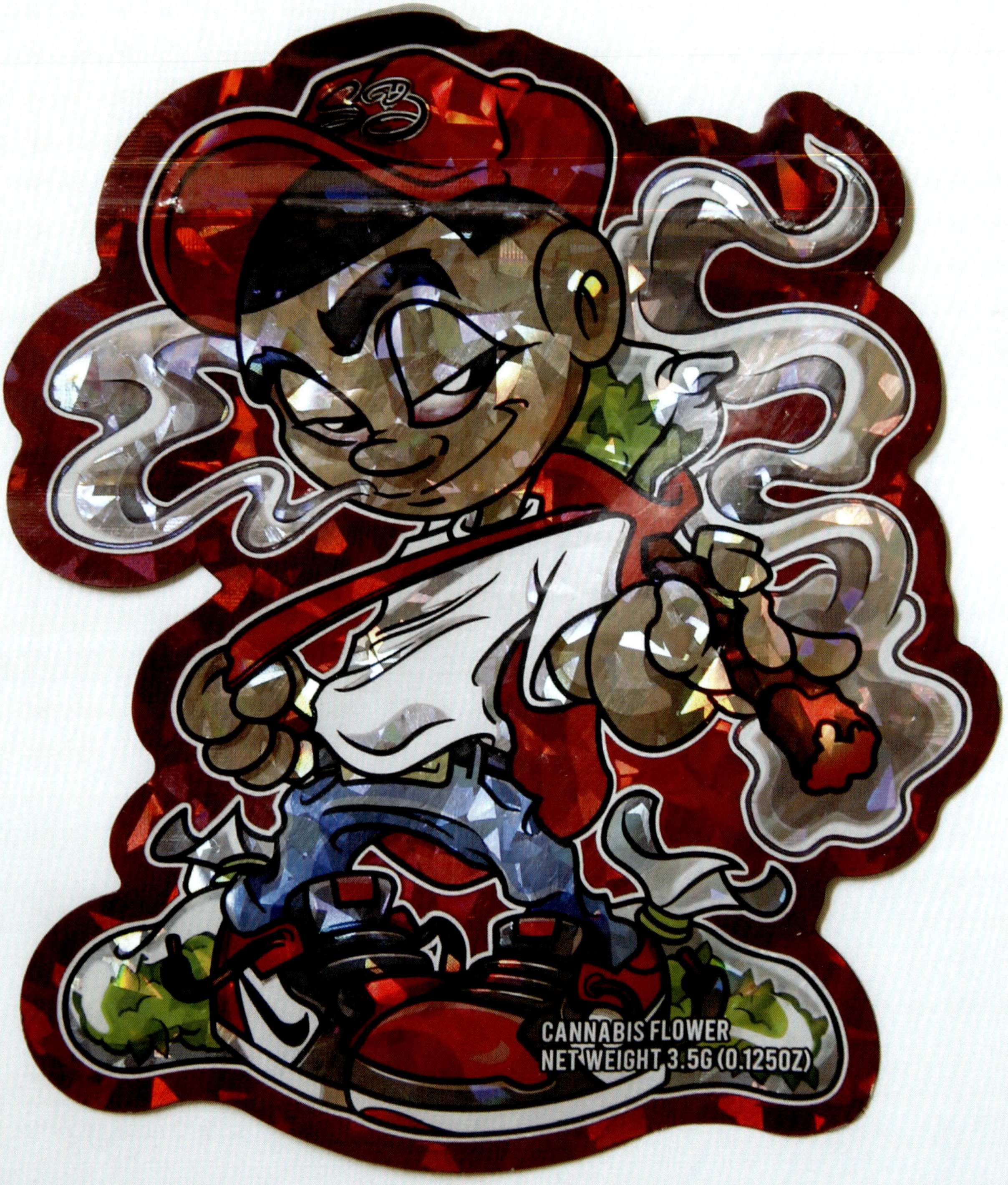
CANNABIS FLOWER
NET WEIGHT 3.5G (0.125OZ)

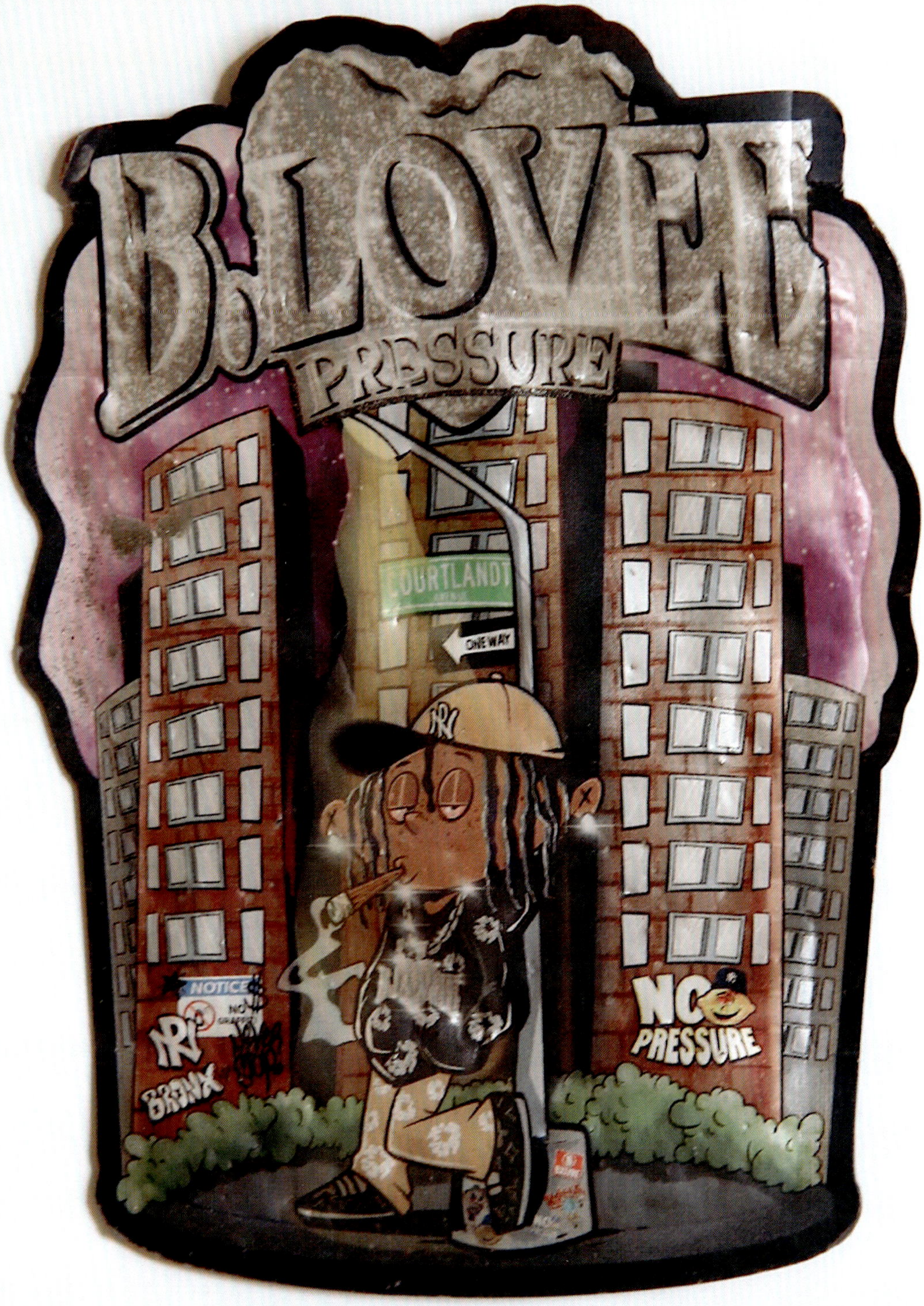
B.LOVEE
PRESSURE
ONE WAY
NOTICE
NO PRESSURE
BRONX

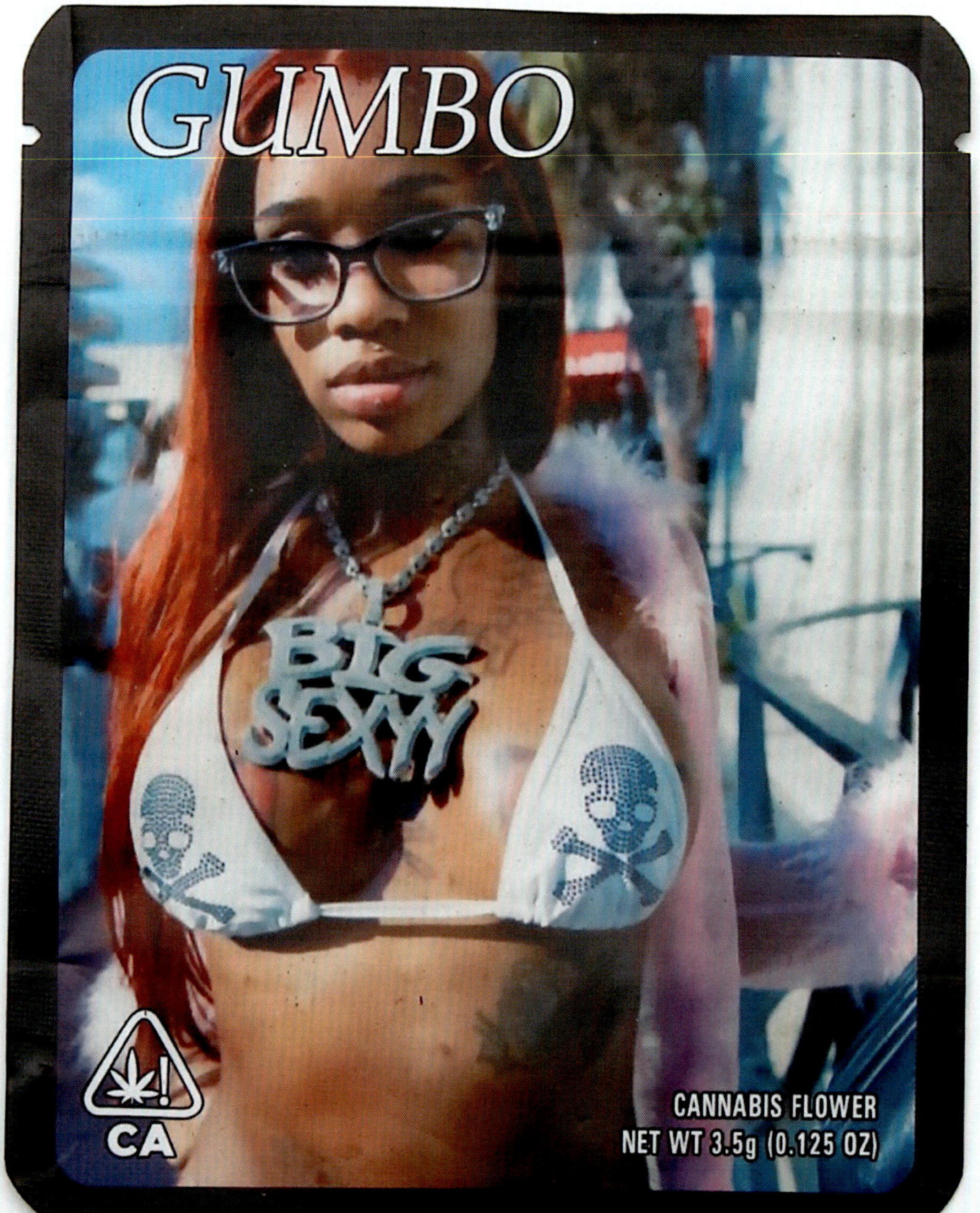
GUMBO
BIG SEXYY
CA
CANNABIS FLOWER
NET WT 3.5g (0.125 OZ)

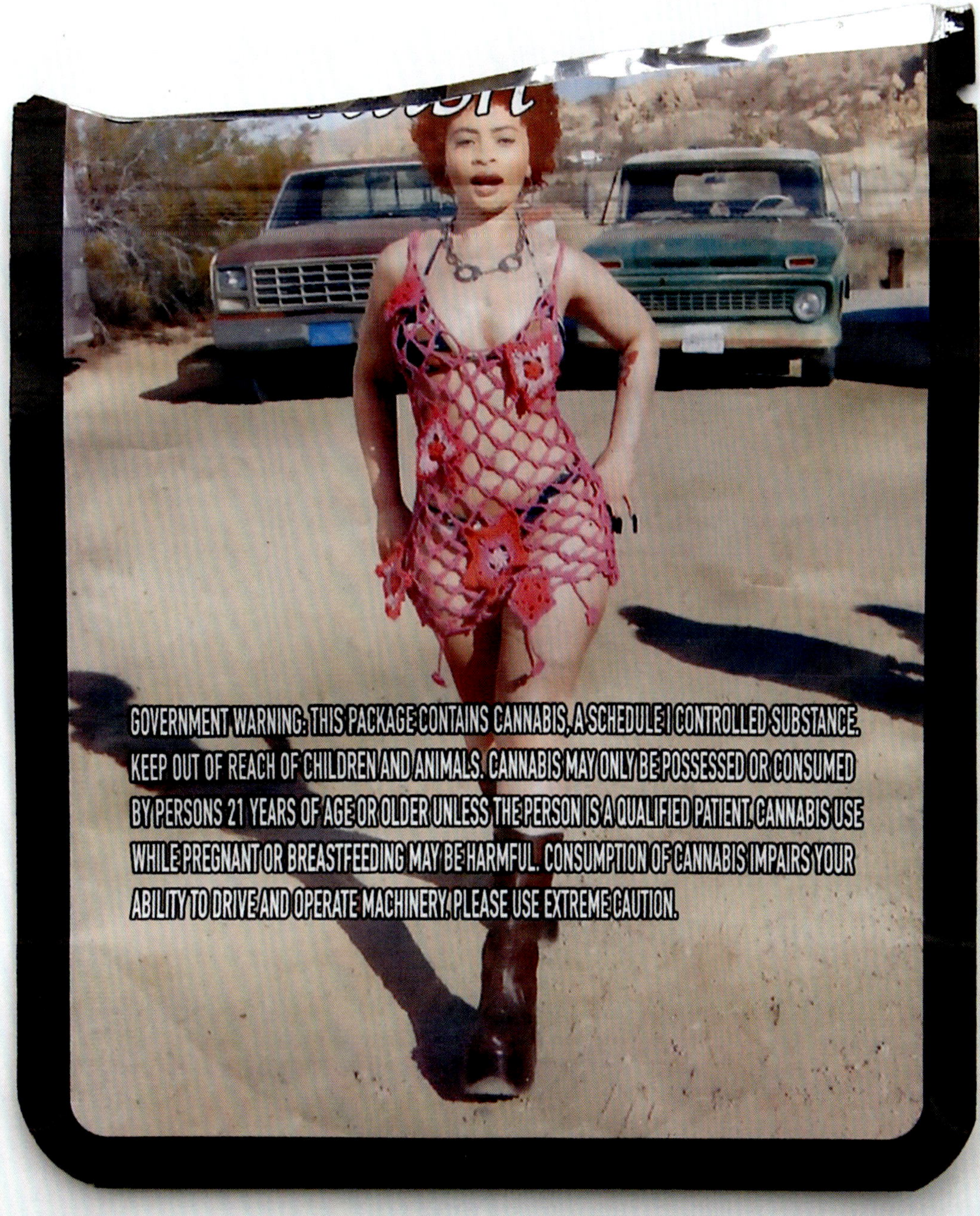
GOVERNMENT WARNING: THIS PACKAGE CONTAINS CANNABIS, A SCHEDULE I CONTROLLED SUBSTANCE. KEEP OUT OF REACH OF CHILDREN AND ANIMALS. CANNABIS MAY ONLY BE POSSESSED OR CONSUMED BY PERSONS 21 YEARS OF AGE OR OLDER UNLESS THE PERSON IS A QUALIFIED PATIENT. CANNABIS USE WHILE PREGNANT OR BREASTFEEDING MAY BE HARMFUL. CONSUMPTION OF CANNABIS IMPAIRS YOUR ABILITY TO DRIVE AND OPERATE MACHINERY. PLEASE USE EXTREME CAUTION.

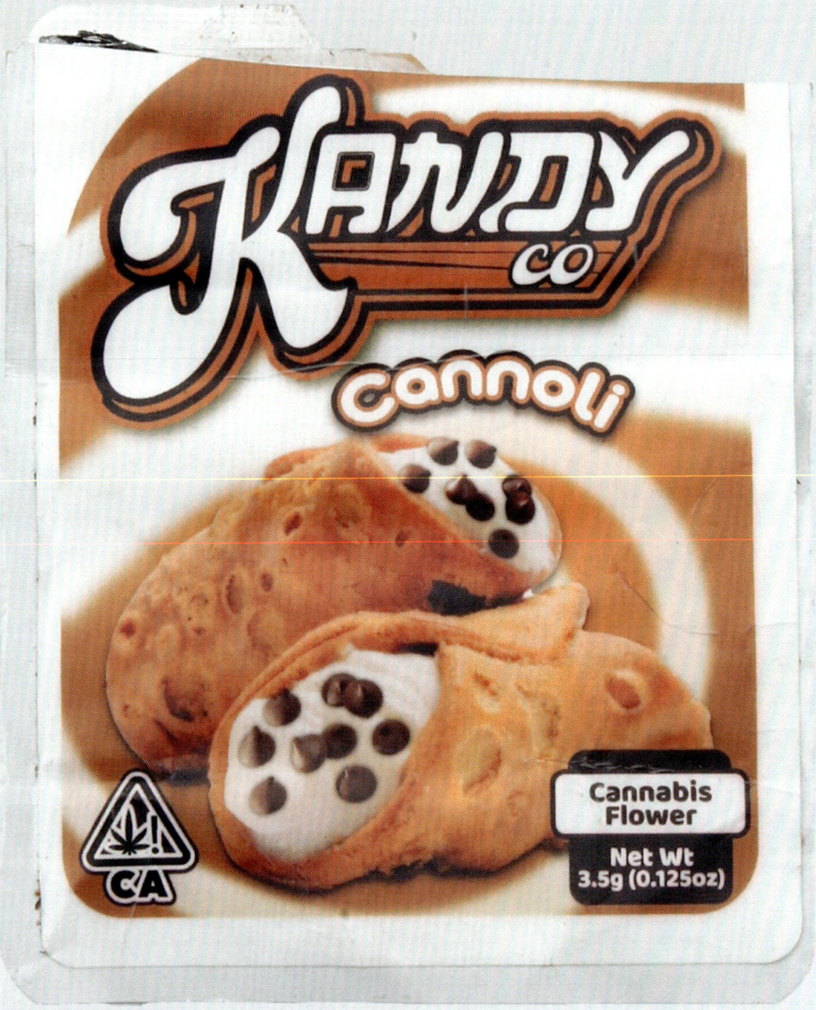
Kandy co
Cannoli
Cannabis Flower
Net Wt 3.5g (0.125oz)
CA

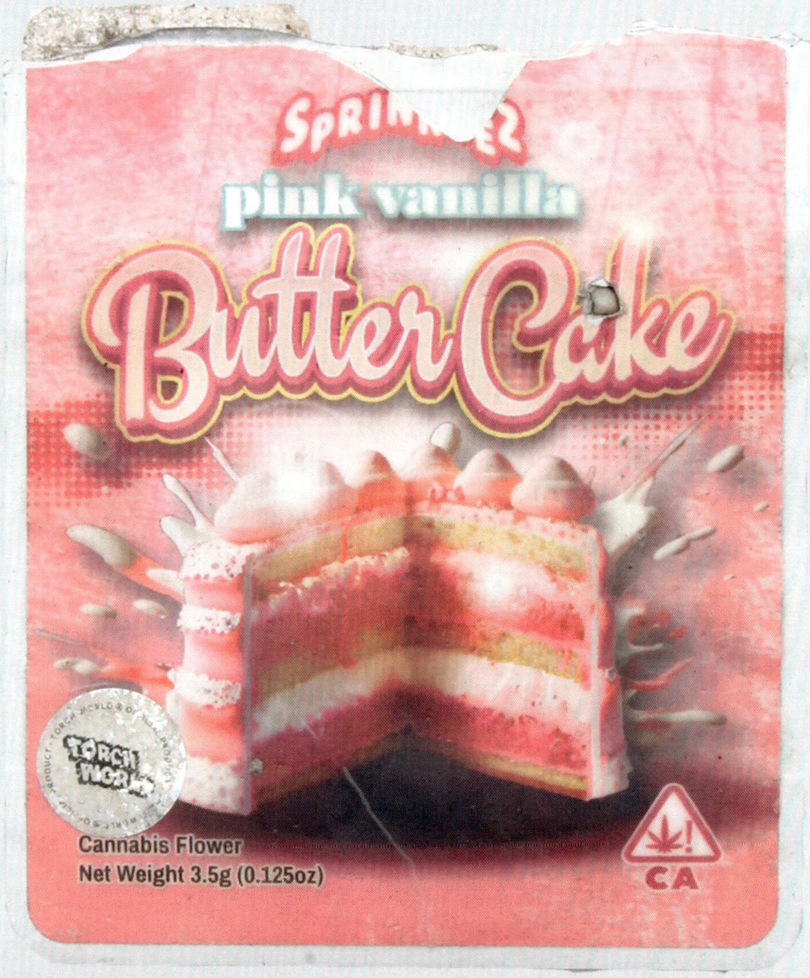
pink vanilla
Butter Cake
Cannabis Flower
Net Weight 3.5g (0.125oz)
CA

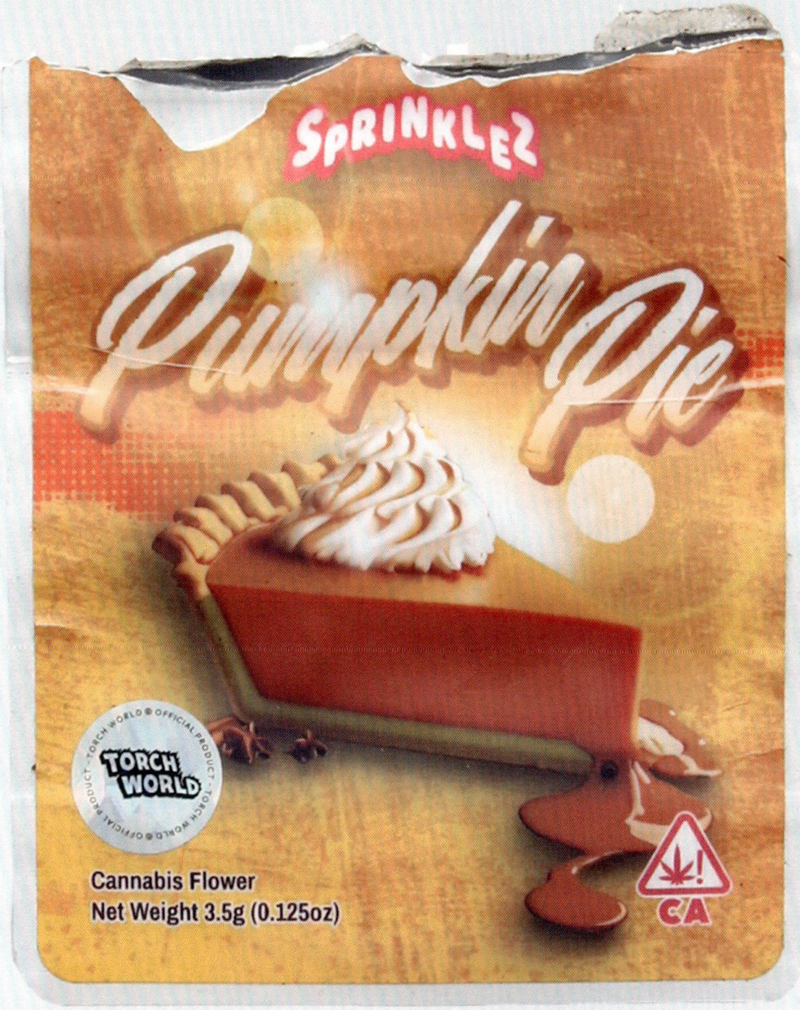
SPRINKLEZ
Pumpkin Pie
TORCH WORLD
Cannabis Flower
Net Weight 3.5g (0.125oz)
CA

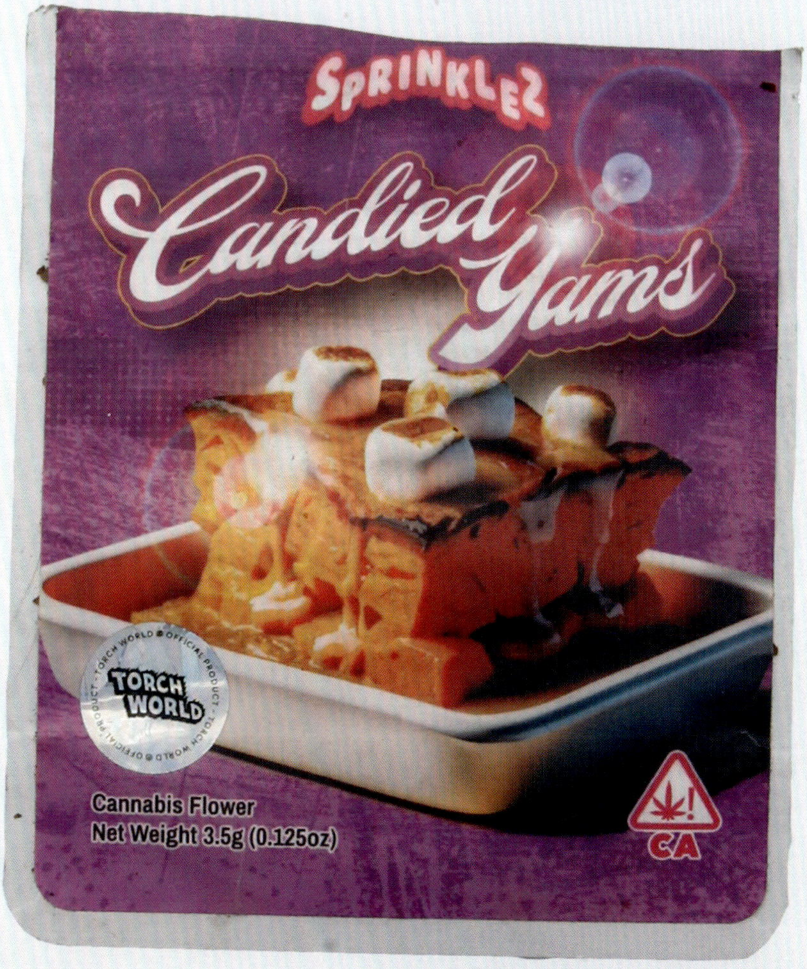
SPRINKLEZ
Candied Yams
TORCH WORLD
Cannabis Flower
Net Weight 3.5g (0.125oz)
CA

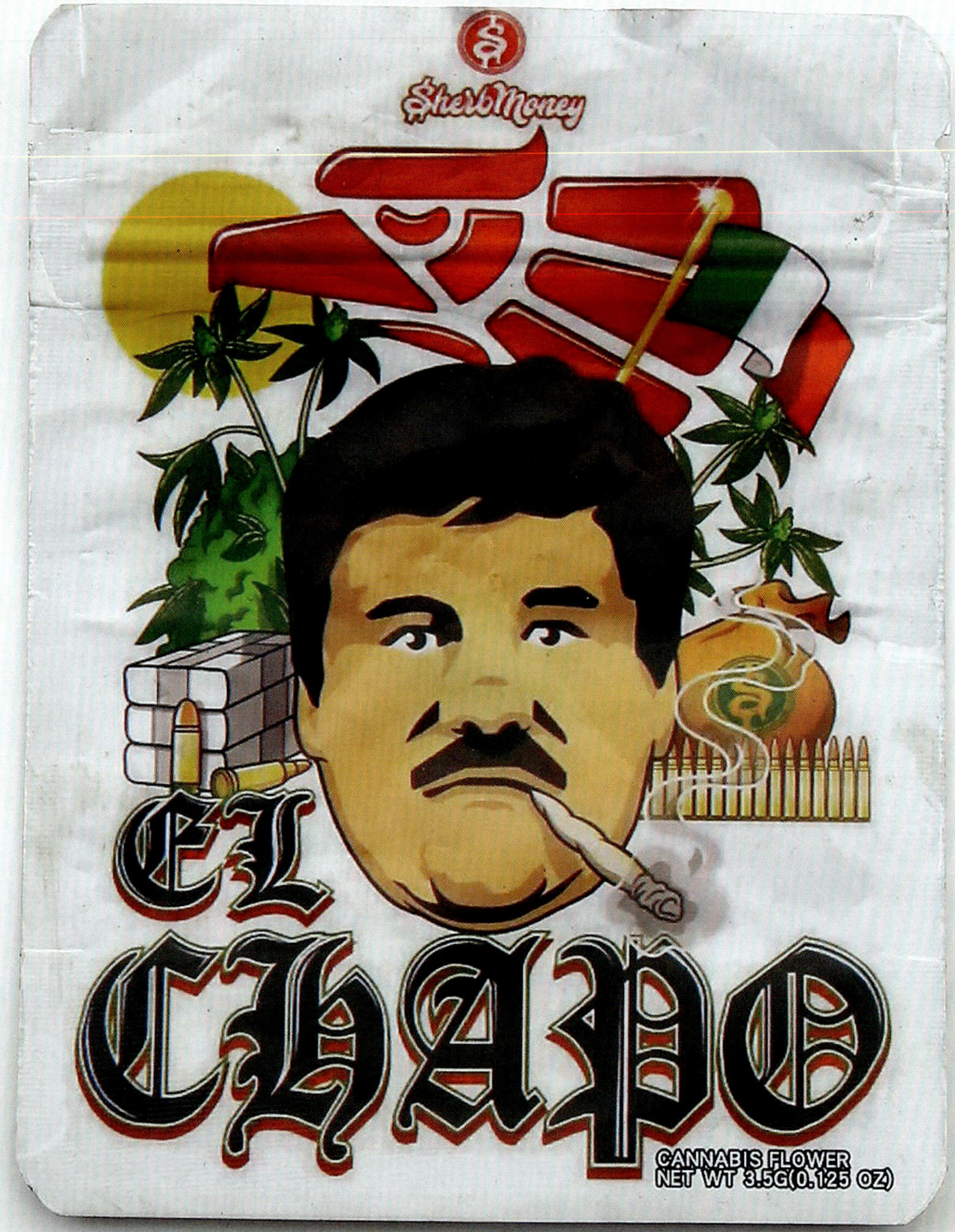
SherbMoney
EL
CHAPO
CANNABIS FLOWER
NET WT 3.5G(0.125 OZ)

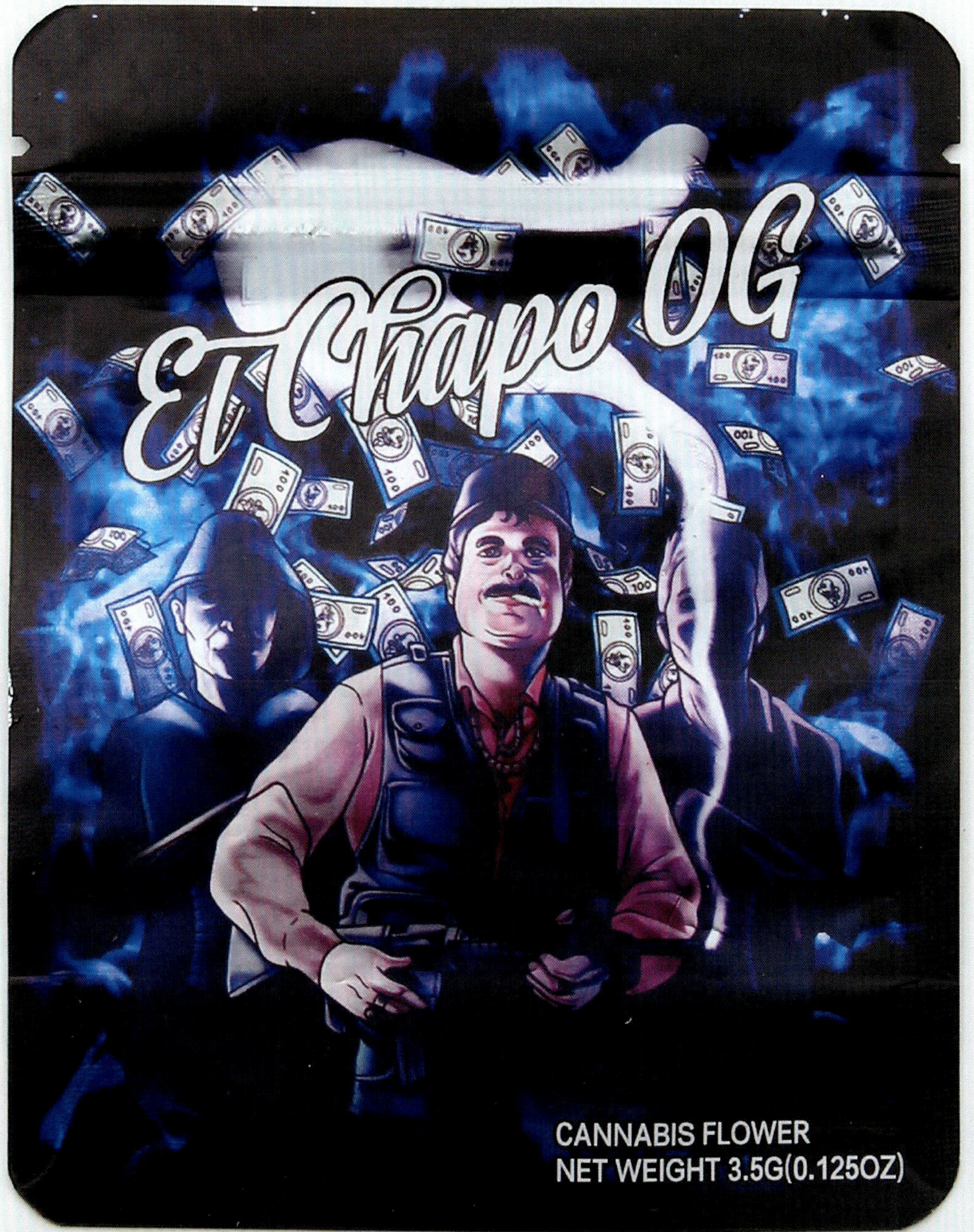
El Chapo OG
CANNABIS FLOWER
NET WEIGHT 3.5G(0.125OZ)

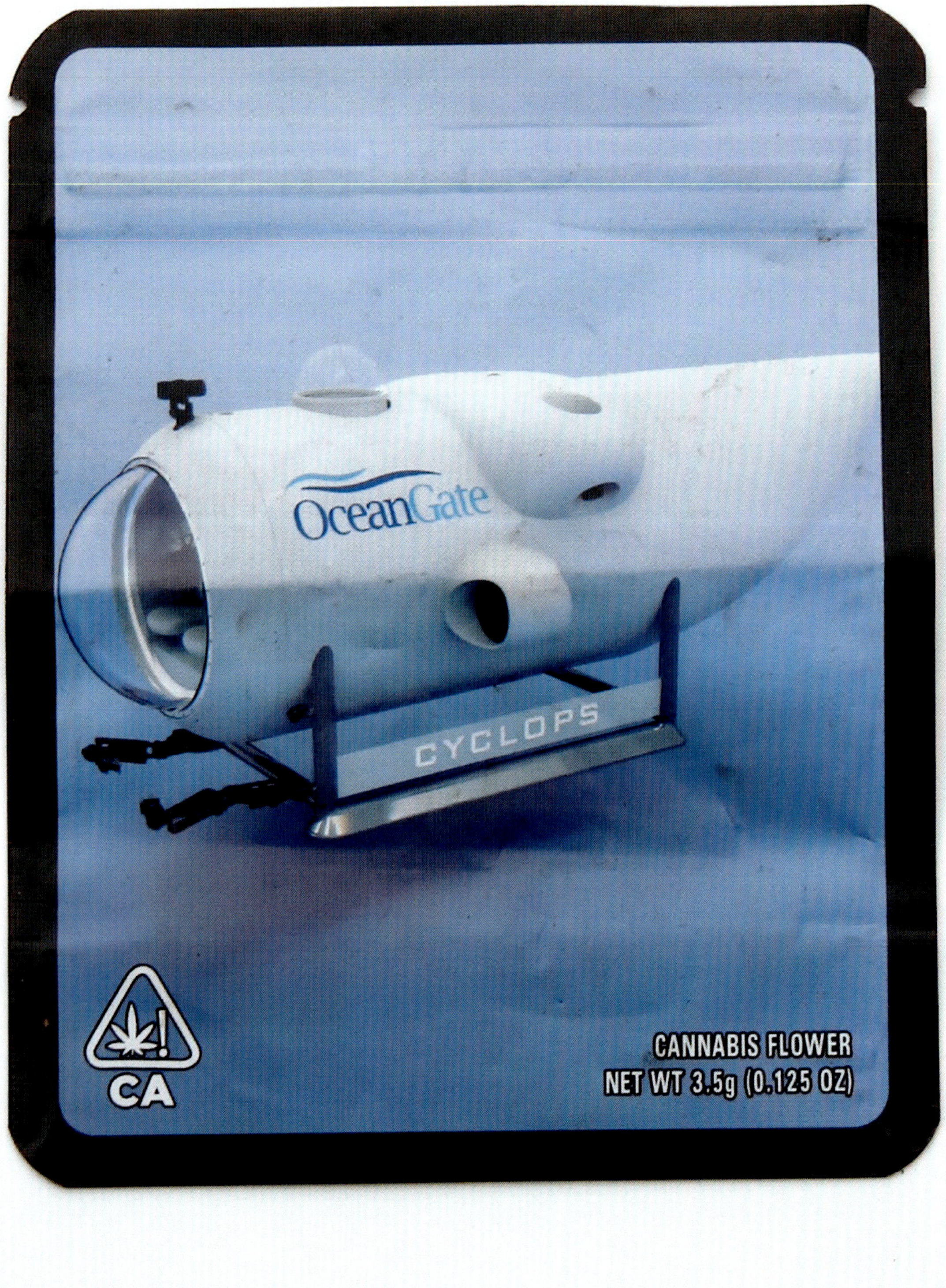
OceanGate
CYCLOPS
CA
CANNABIS FLOWER
NET WT 3.5g (0.125 OZ)

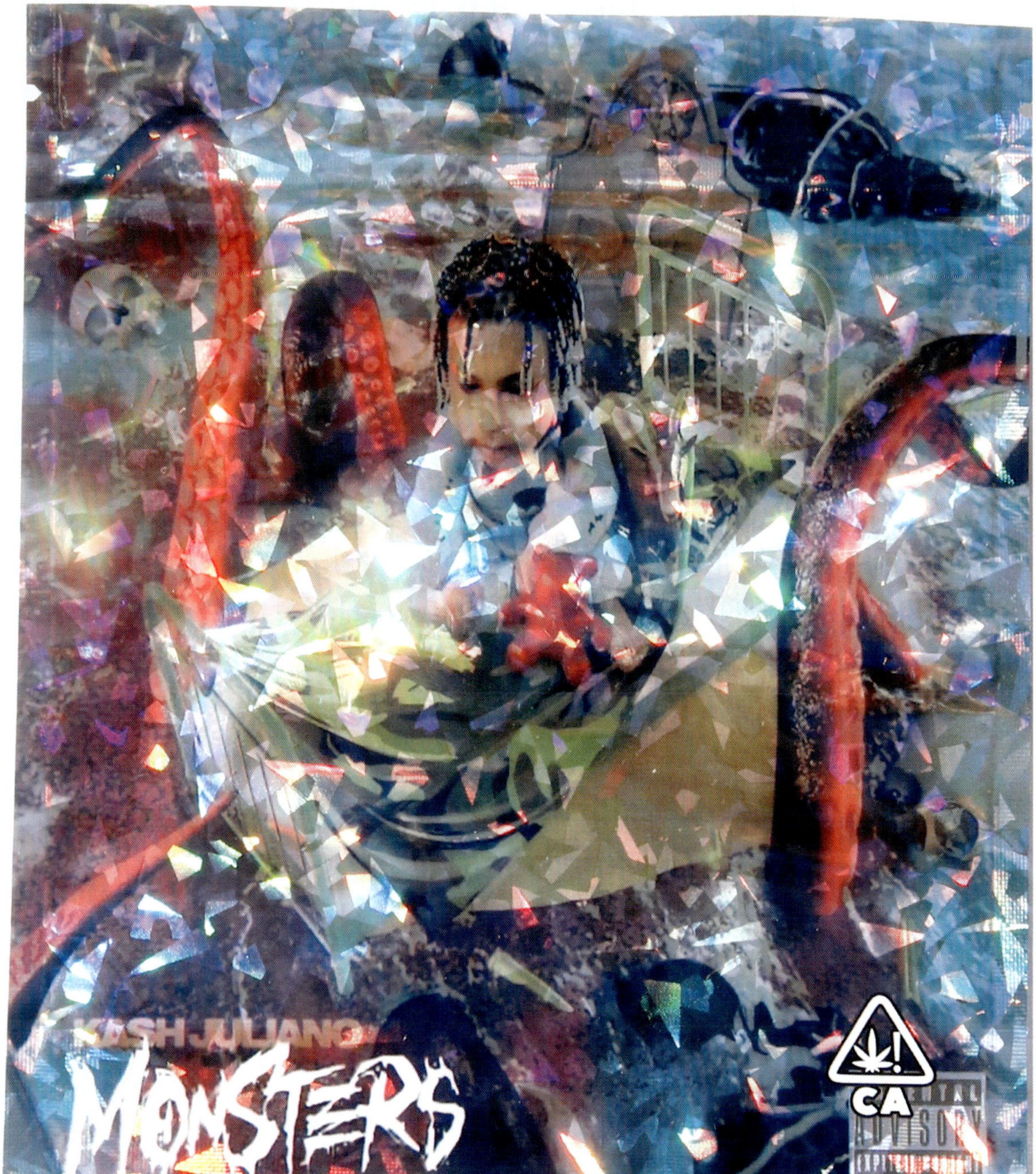
KASH JULIANO
MONSTERS
CA

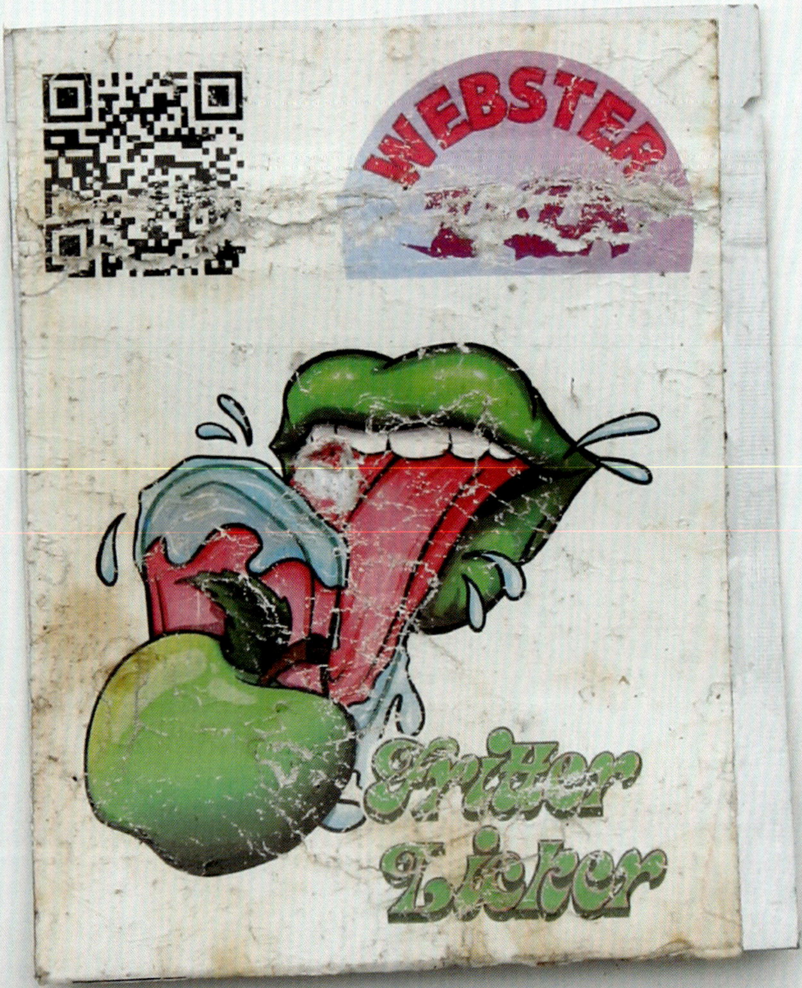
WEBSTER
Fritter Licker

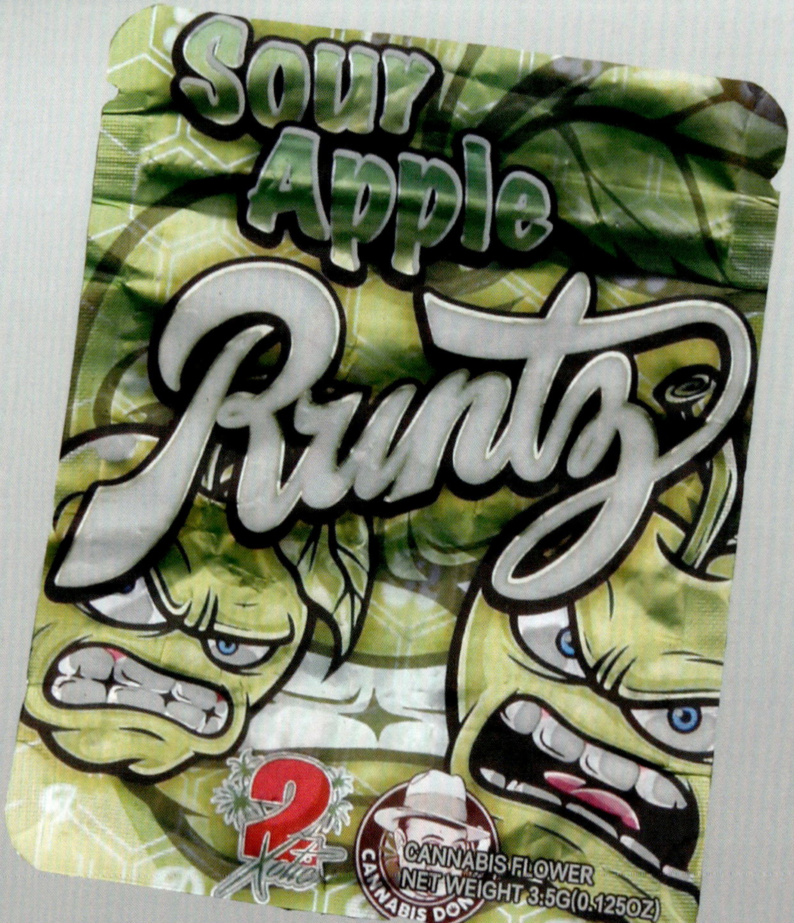
Sour Apple
Runtz
CANNABIS FLOWER
NET WEIGHT 3.5G(0.125OZ)
CANNABIS DON

NOT GUILTY
NOT GUILTY
CA

SPRAY PAINT
NOT GUILTY
Urban Terpz
CA

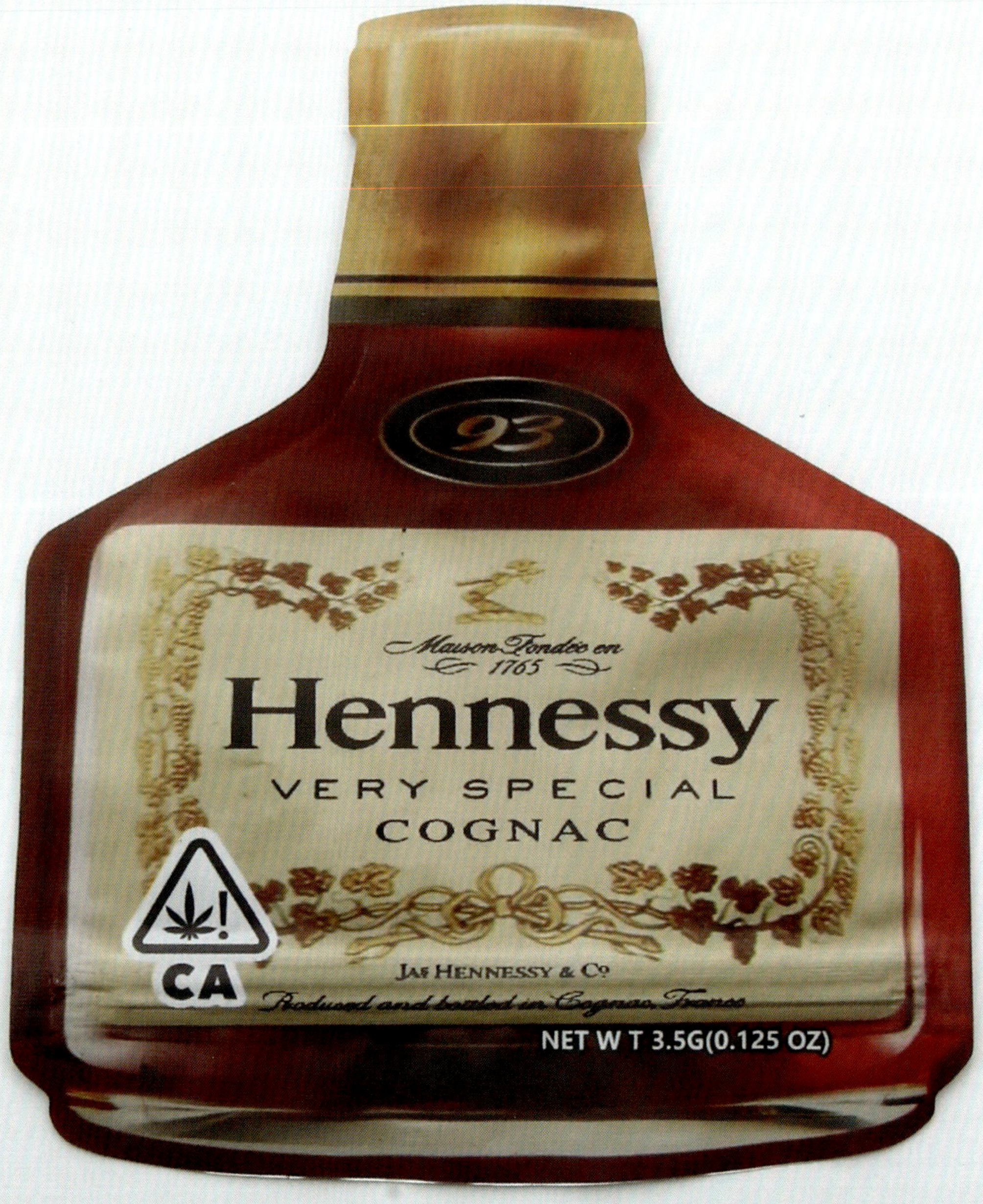
93
Maison Fondée en
1765
Hennessy
VERY SPECIAL
COGNAC
CA
JAS HENNESSY & CO
Produced and bottled in Cognac, France
NET W T 3.5G(0.125 OZ)

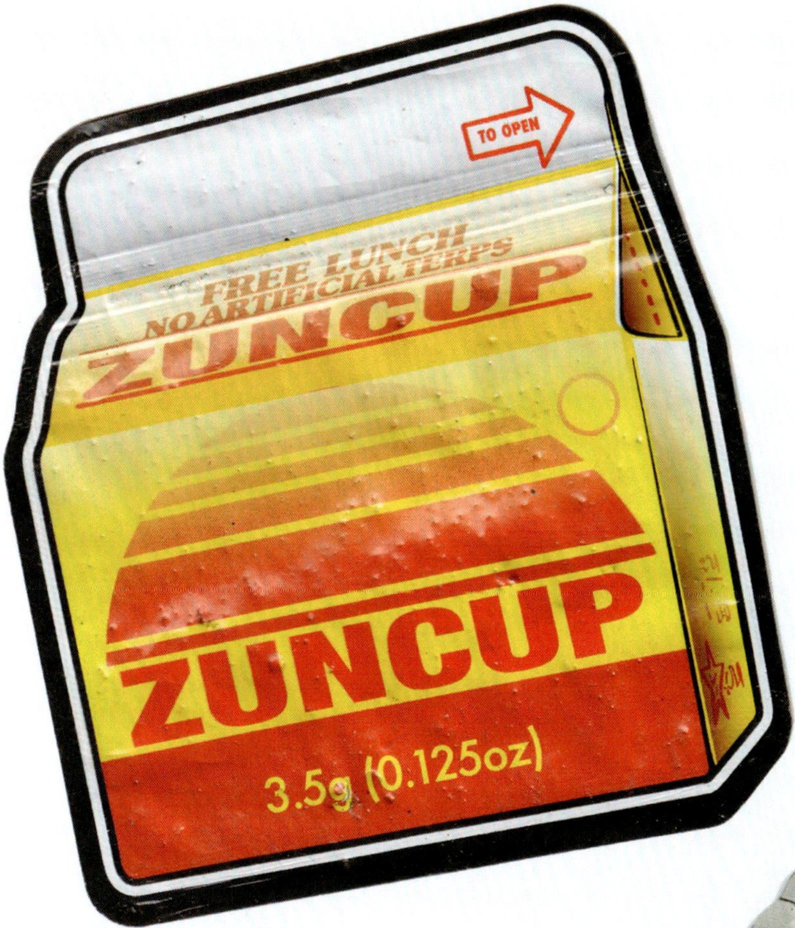
TO OPEN
FREE LUNCH
NO ARTIFICIAL TERPS
ZUNCUP
ZUNCUP
3.5g (0.125oz)

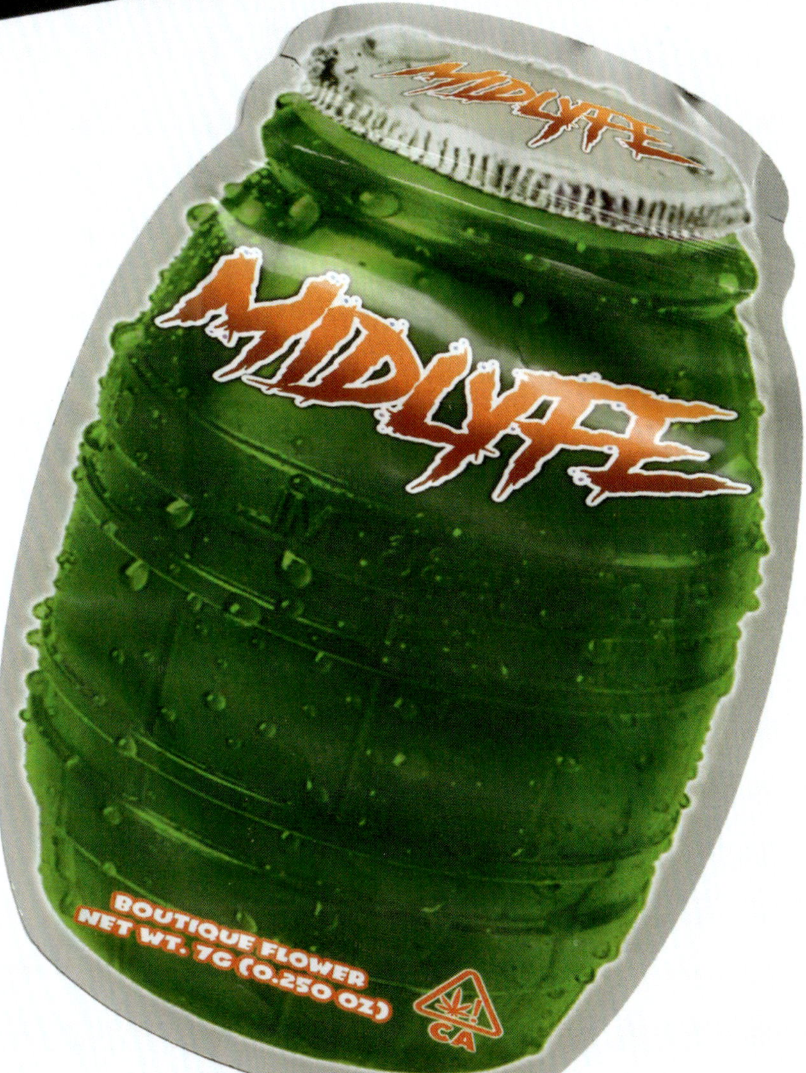
MIDLYFE
MIDLYFE
BOUTIQUE FLOWER
NET WT. 7G (0.250 OZ)
CA

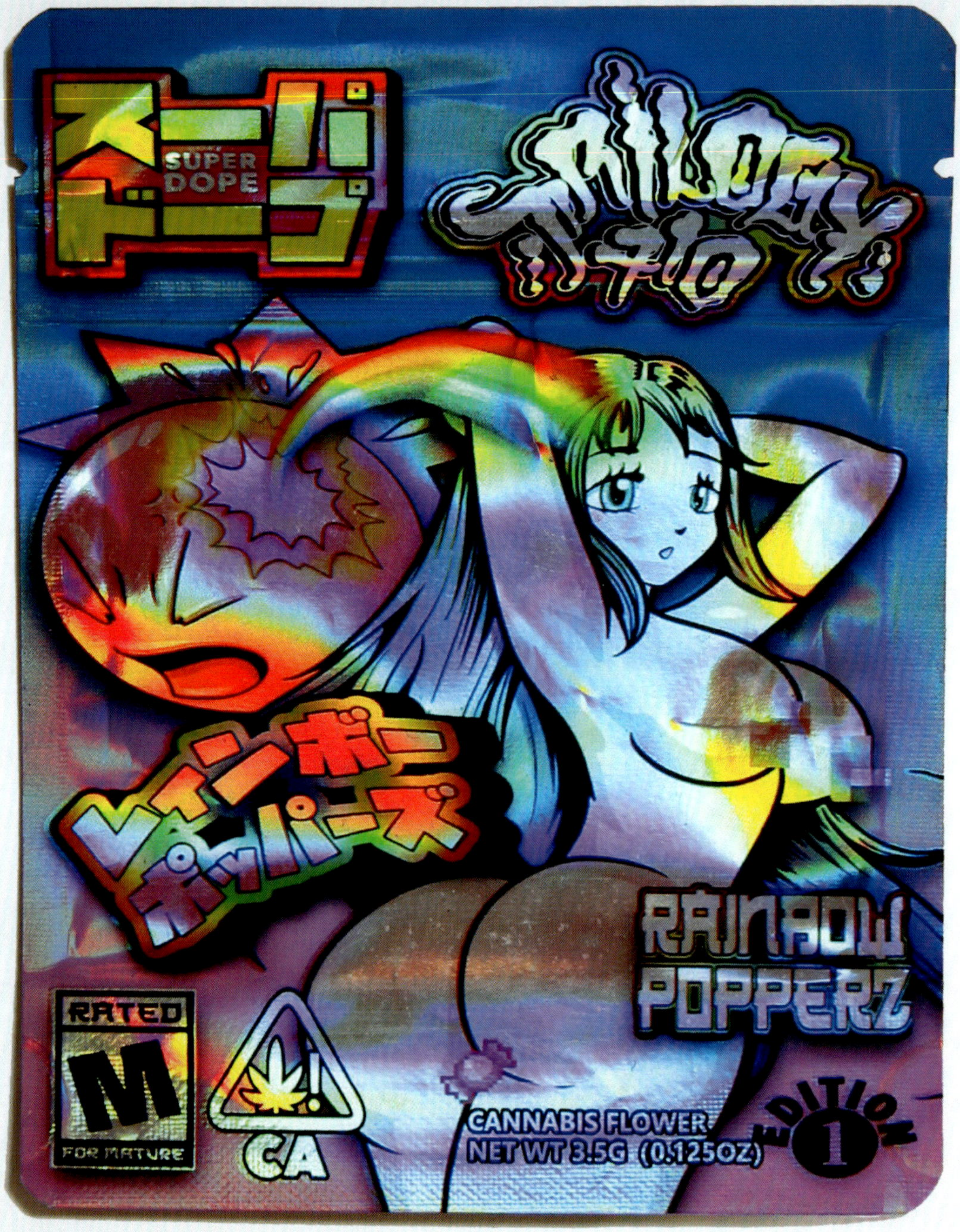
スーパードープ
SUPER DOPE
レインボーポッパーズ
RAINBOW POPPERZ
RATED M FOR MATURE
CA
CANNABIS FLOWER
NET WT 3.5G (0.125OZ)
EDITION 1

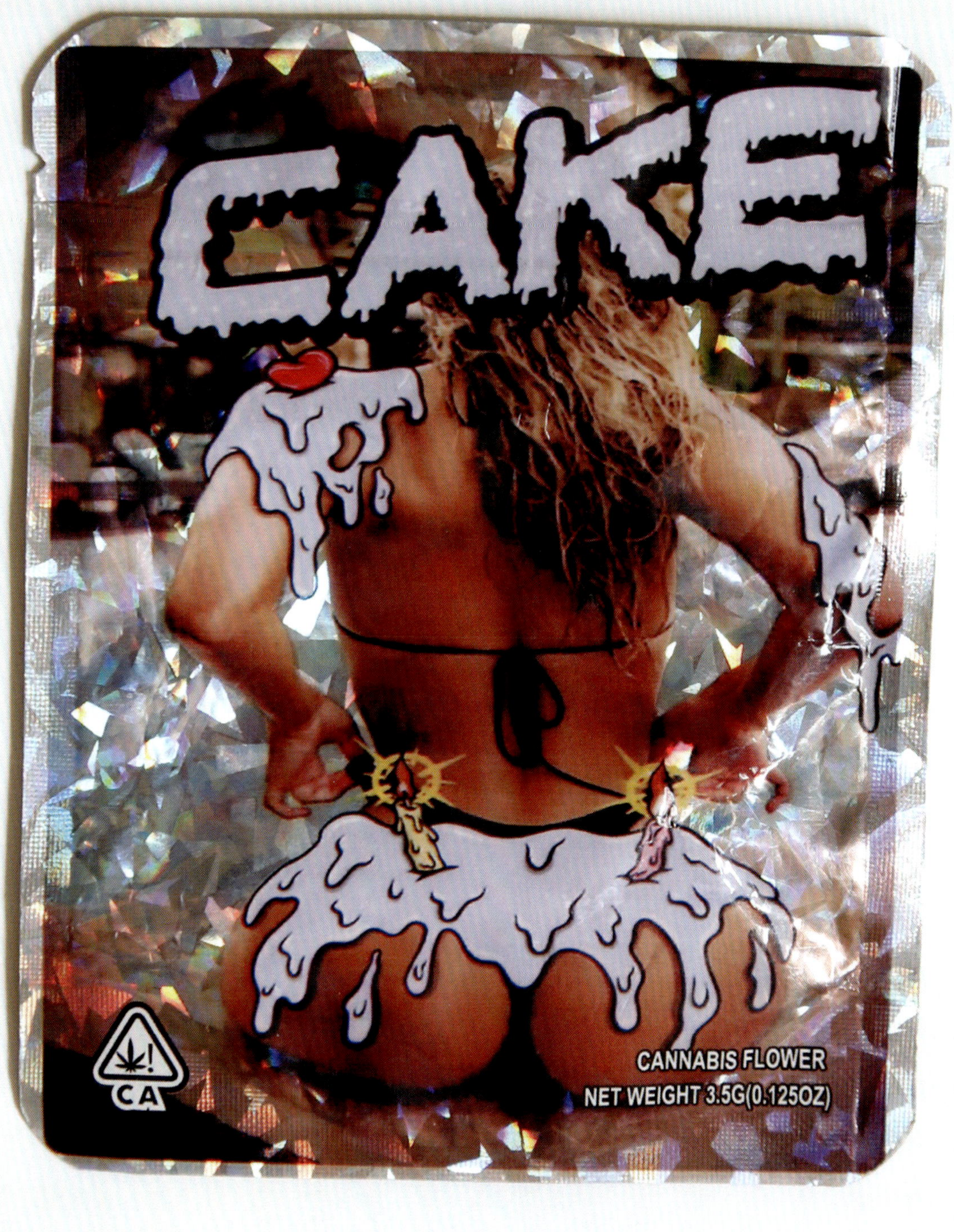
CAKE
CA
CANNABIS FLOWER
NET WEIGHT 3.5G(0.125OZ)

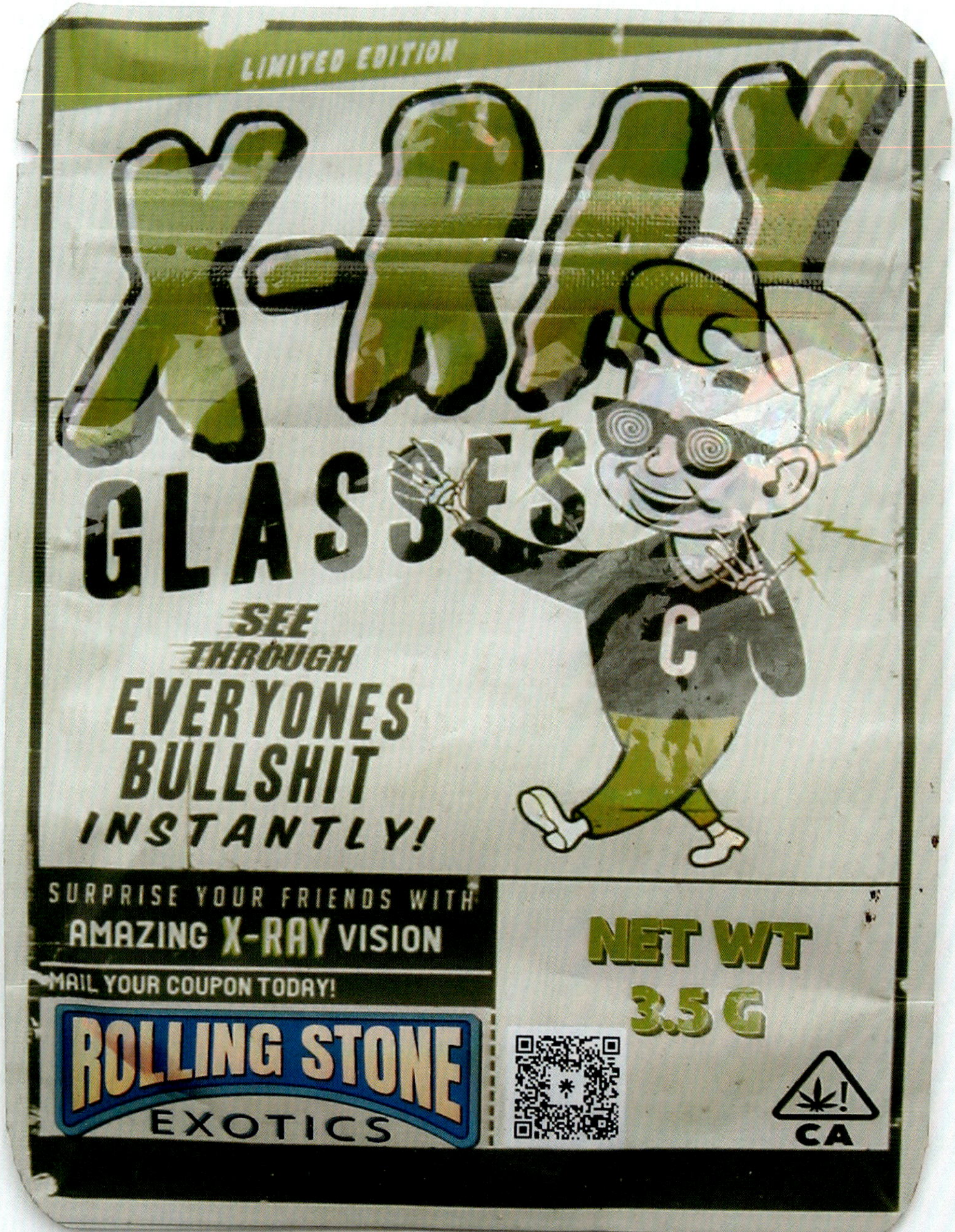
LIMITED EDITION
X-RAY
GLASSES
SEE THROUGH EVERYONES BULLSHIT INSTANTLY!
SURPRISE YOUR FRIENDS WITH
AMAZING X-RAY VISION
MAIL YOUR COUPON TODAY!
ROLLING STONE
EXOTICS
NET WT
3.5 G
CA

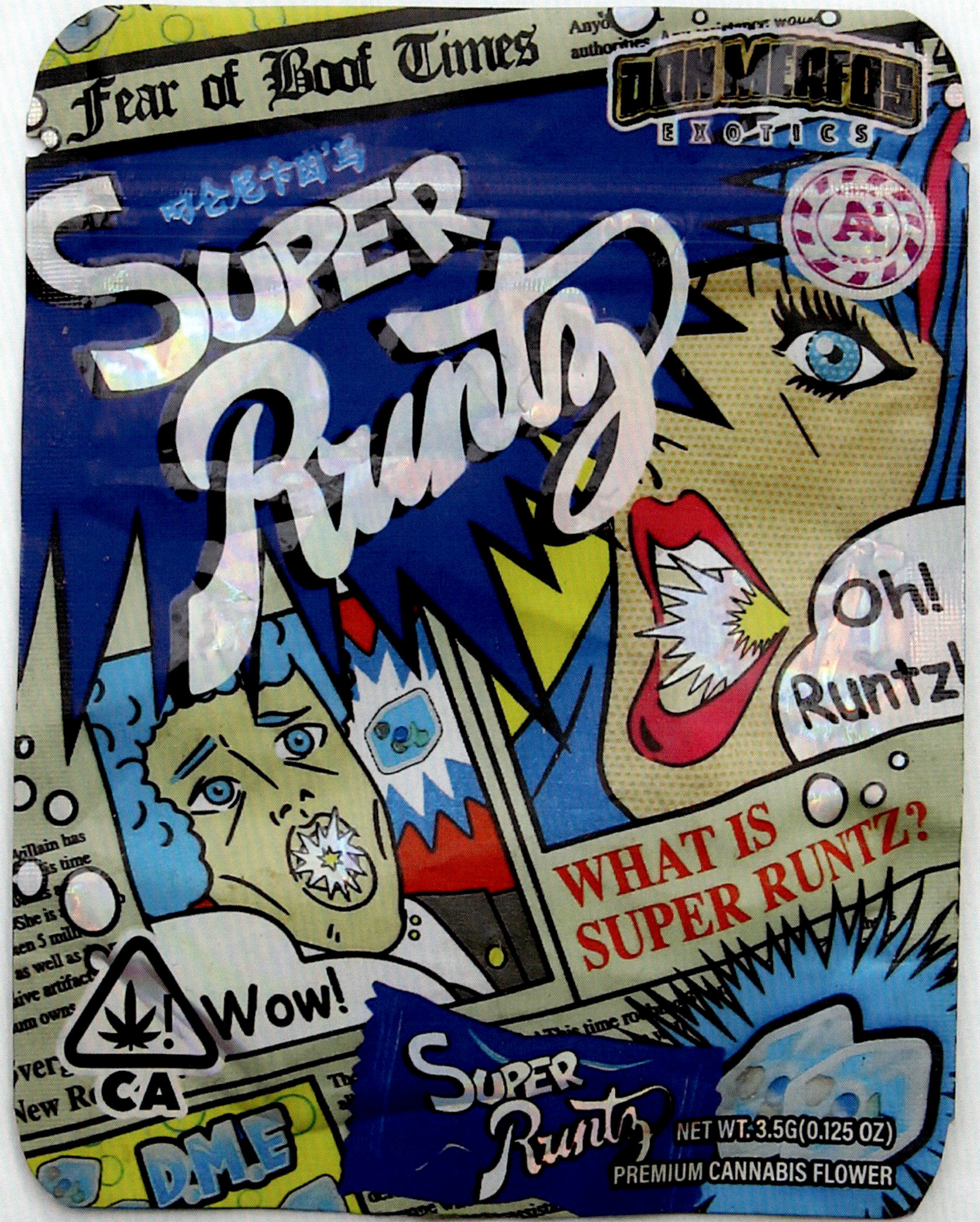
Fear of Boof Times
SUPER Runtz
Oh! Runtz!
WHAT IS SUPER RUNTZ?
Wow!
CA
D.M.E
Super Runtz
NET WT. 3.5G(0.125 OZ)
PREMIUM CANNABIS FLOWER

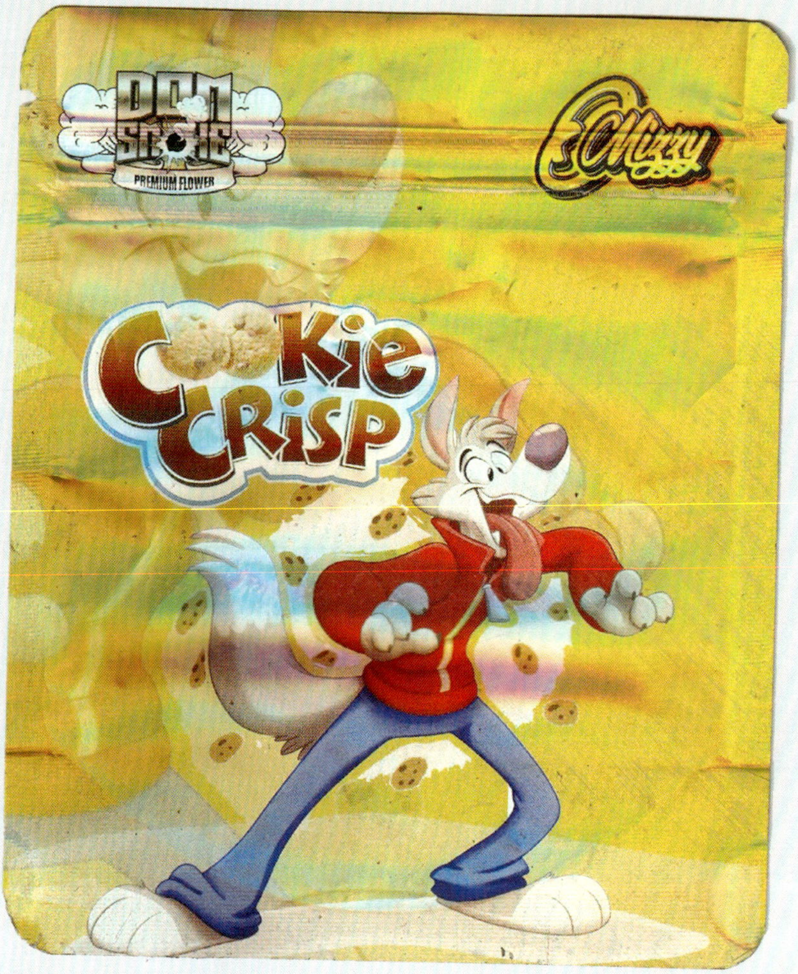
PREMIUM FLOWER
Cookie Crisp

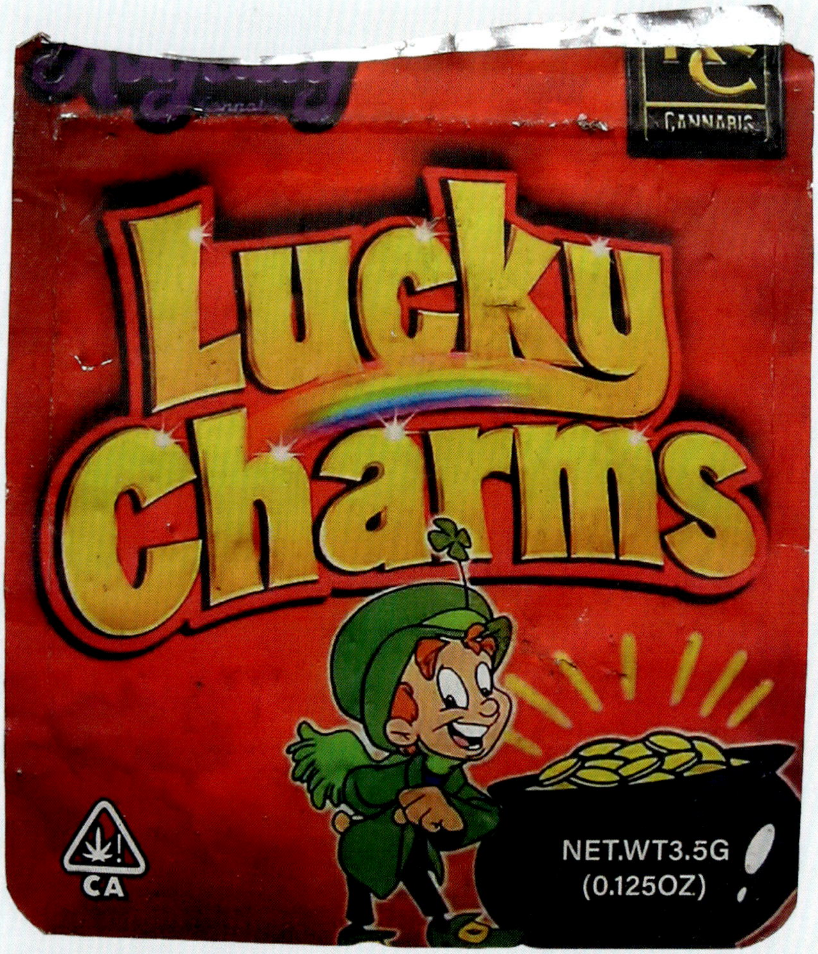
CANNABIS
Lucky Charms
CA
NET.WT3.5G
(0.125OZ)

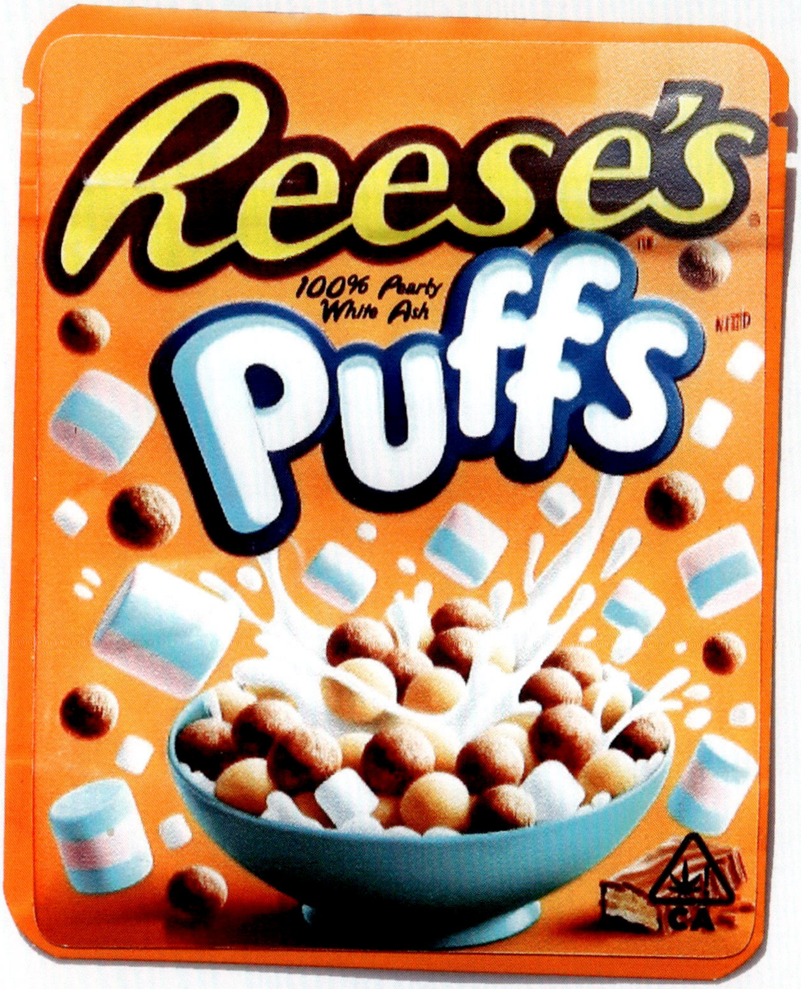
Reese's
100% Pearly White Ash
Puffs
CA

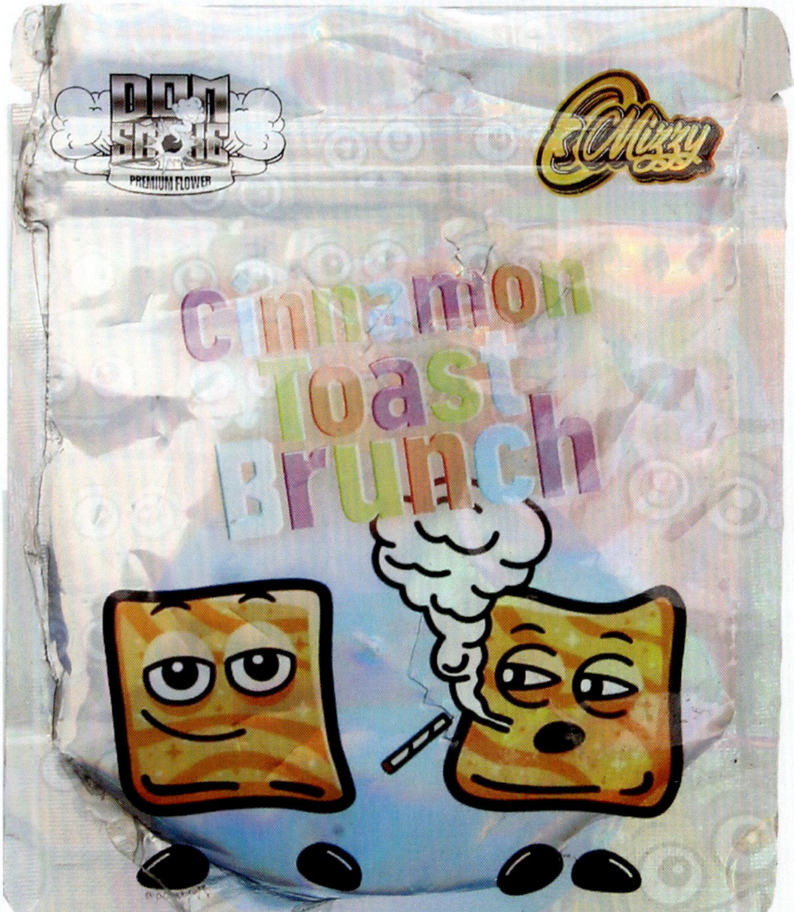
PREMIUM FLOWER
Cinnamon
Toast
Brunch

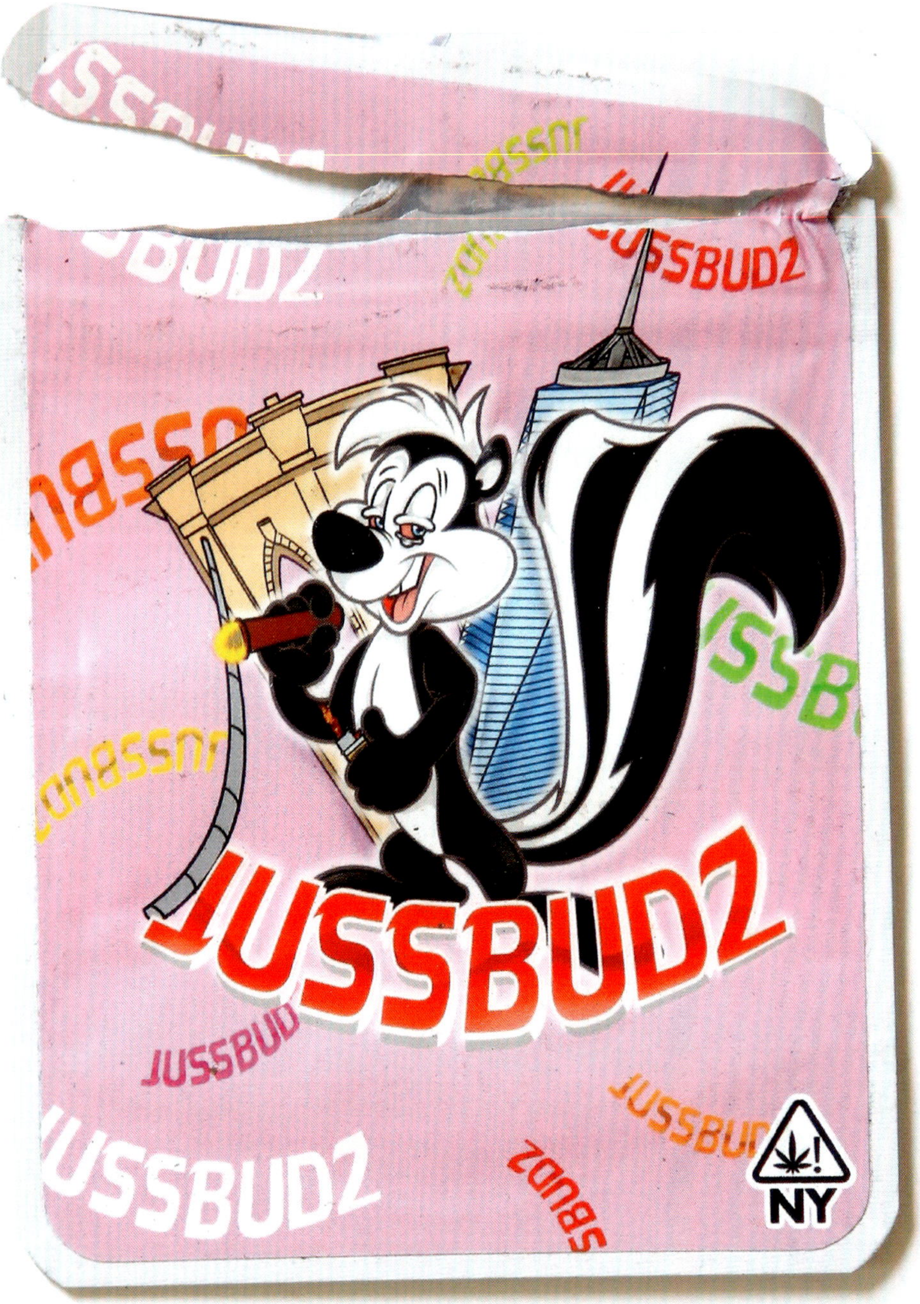
JUSSBUDZ
USSBUDZ
USSBUDZ
JUSSBUD
JUSSBUD
NY

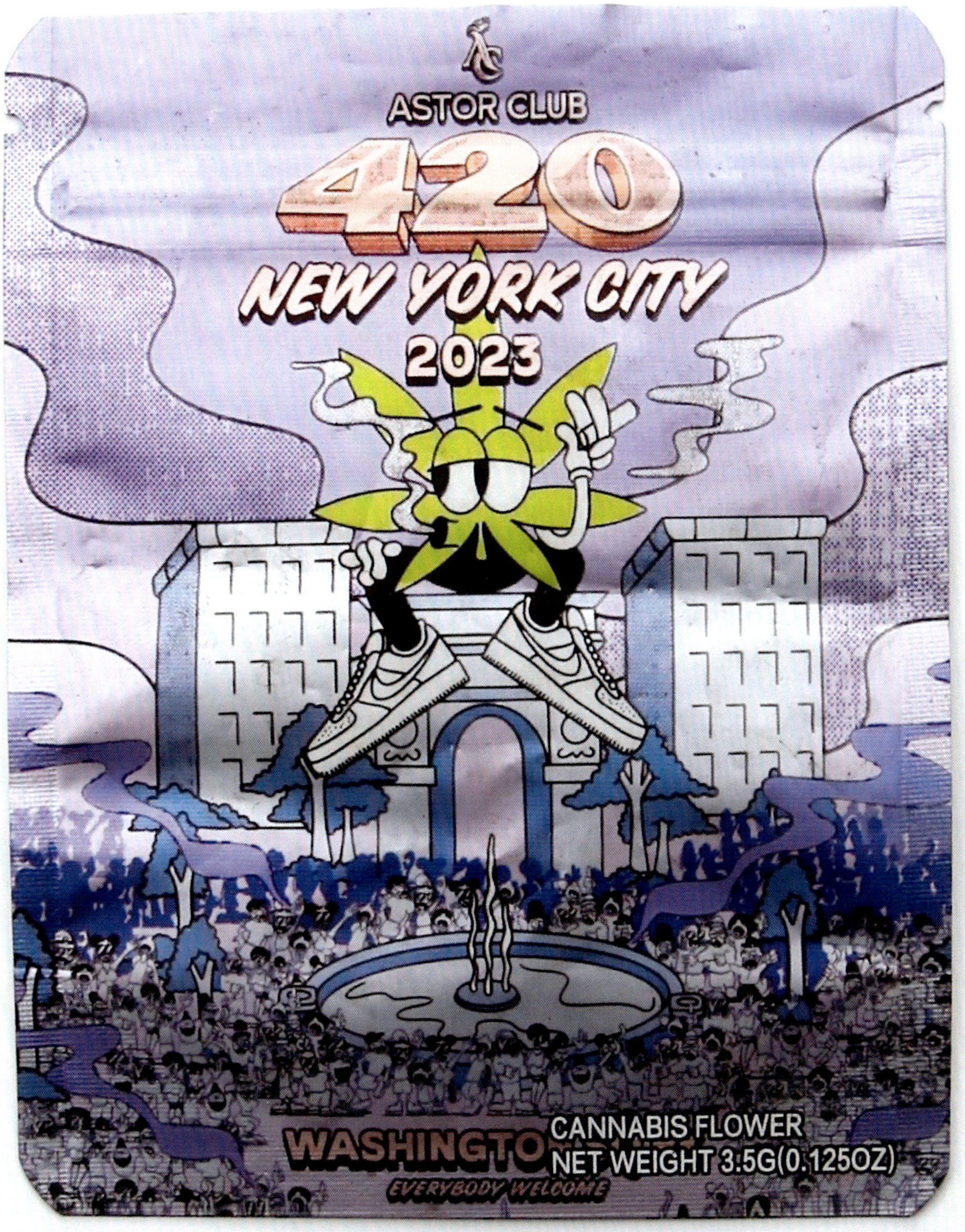
ASTOR CLUB
420
NEW YORK CITY
2023
WASHINGTO
CANNABIS FLOWER
NET WEIGHT 3.5G(0.125OZ)
EVERYBODY WELCOME

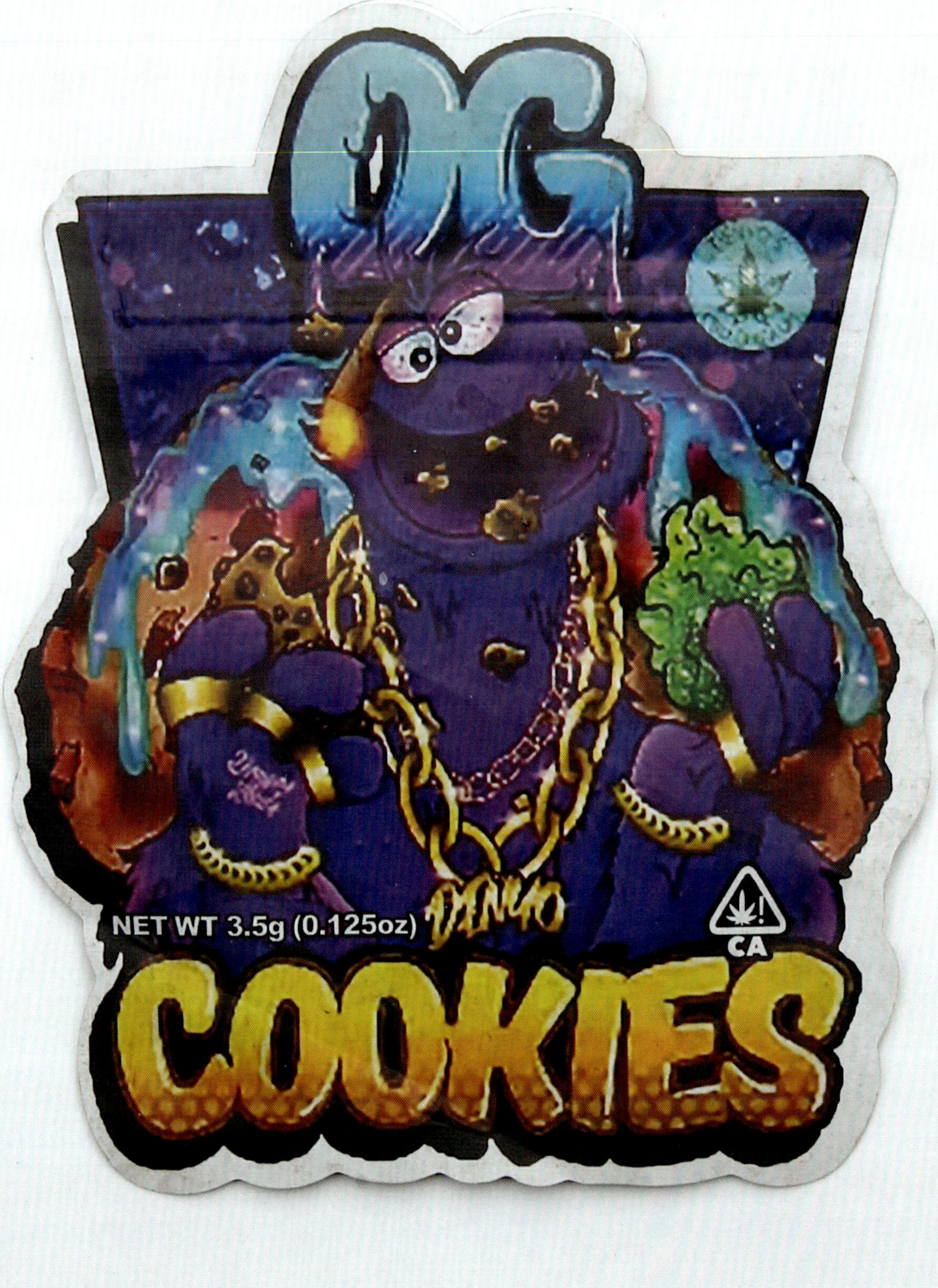
OG
NET WT 3.5g (0.125oz)
CA
COOKIES

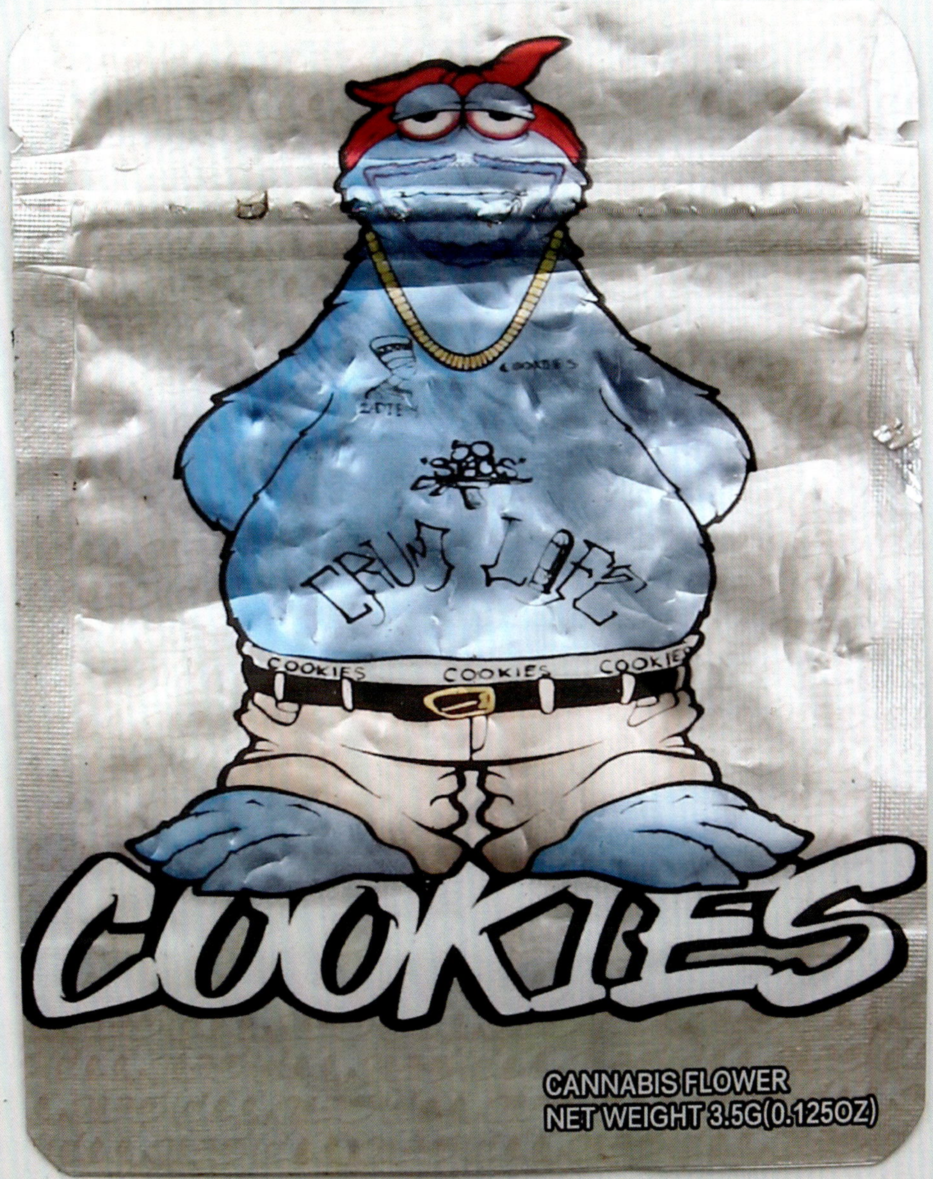
COOKIES
CANNABIS FLOWER
NET WEIGHT 3.5G(0.125OZ)

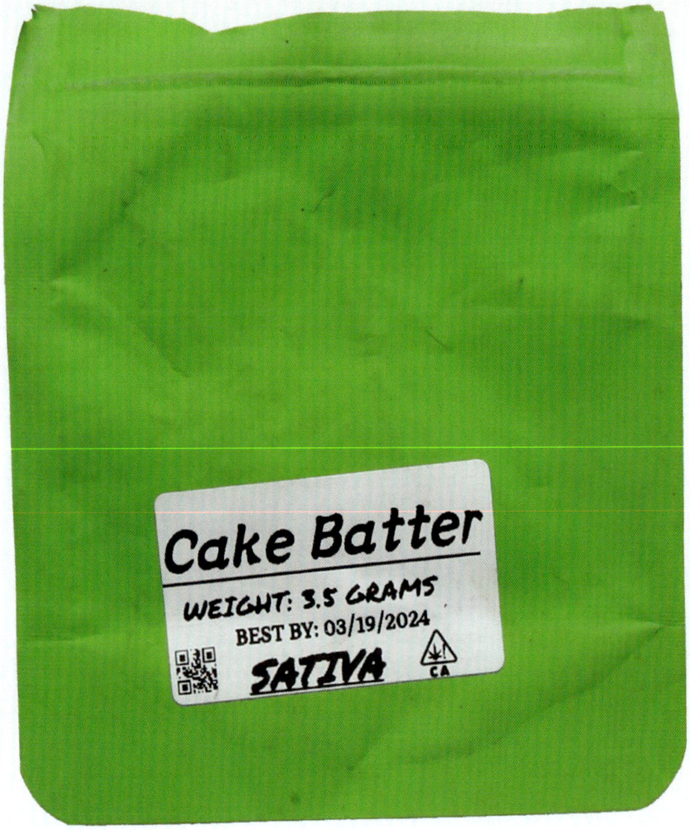
Cake Batter
WEIGHT: 3.5 GRAMS
BEST BY: 03/19/2024
SATIVA
CA

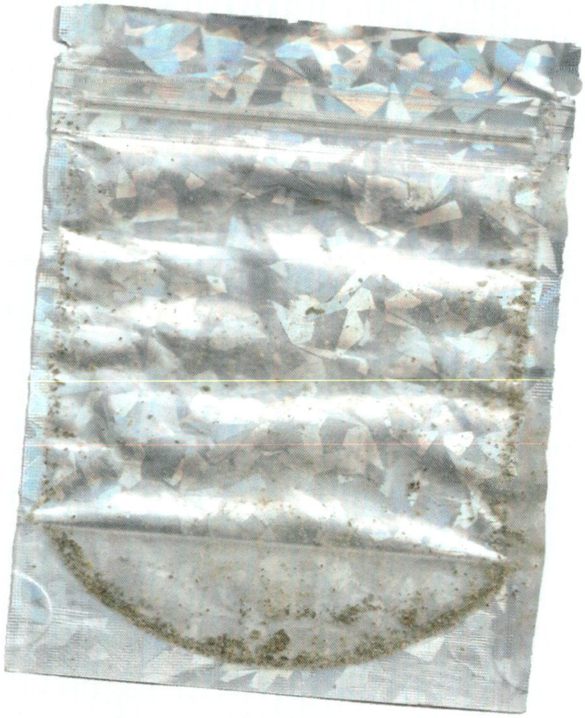

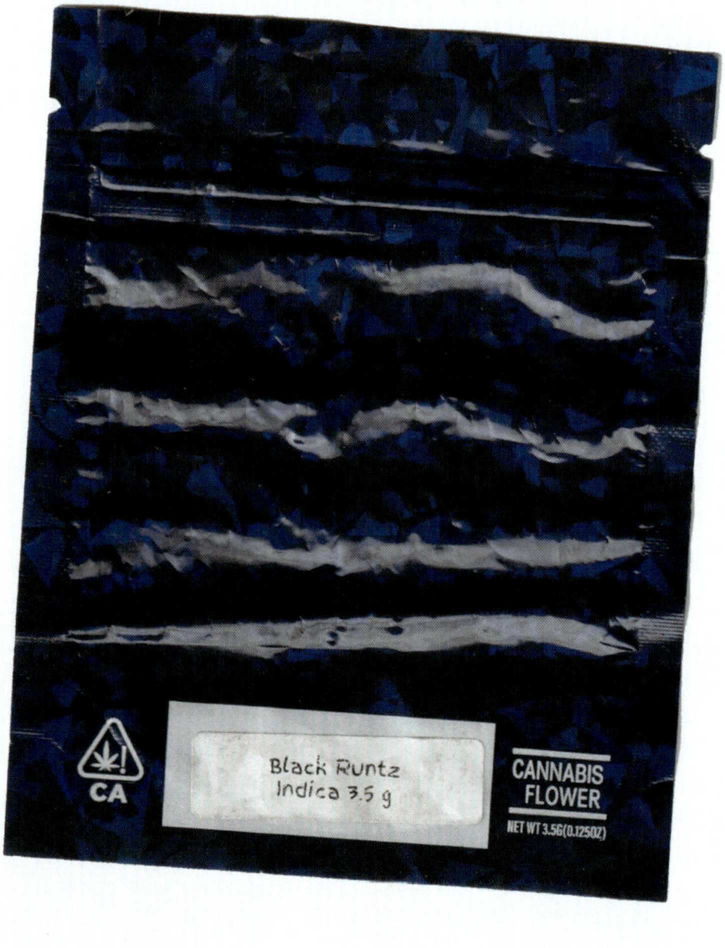
CA
Black Runtz
Indica 3.5 g
CANNABIS
FLOWER
NET WT 3.5G(0.125OZ)

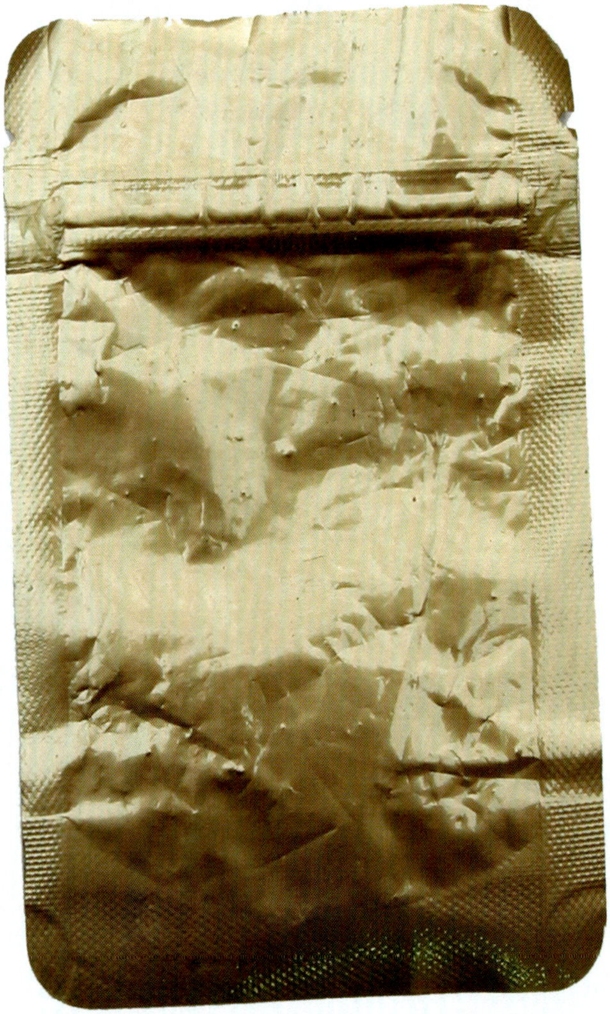

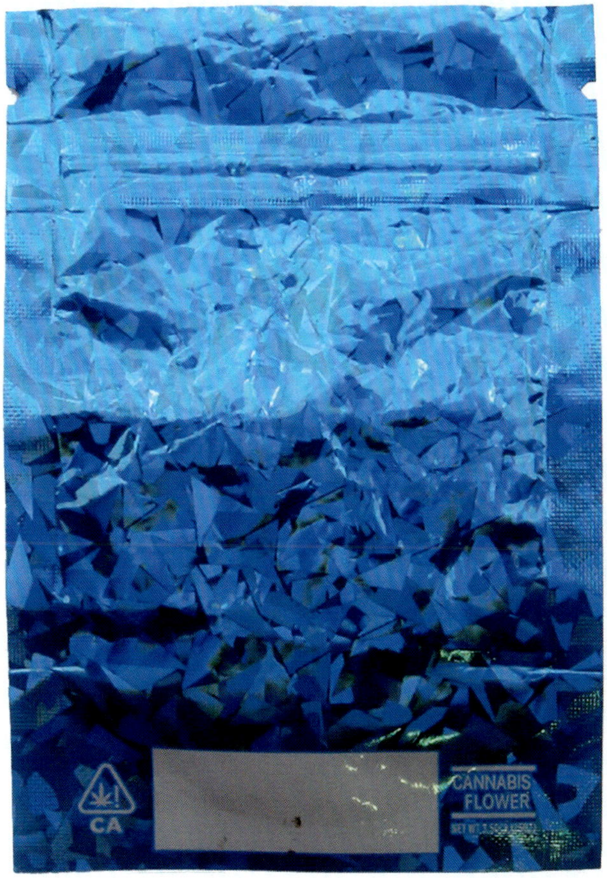
CA
CANNABIS FLOWER

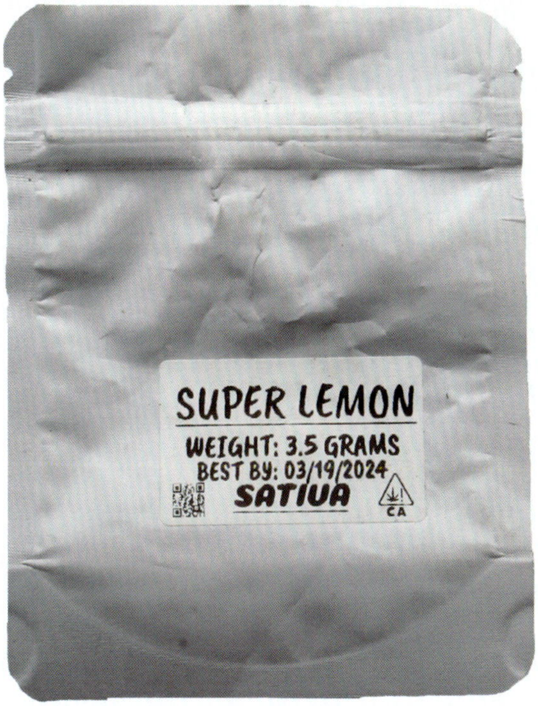
SUPER LEMON
WEIGHT: 3.5 GRAMS
BEST BY: 03/19/2024
SATIVA
CA

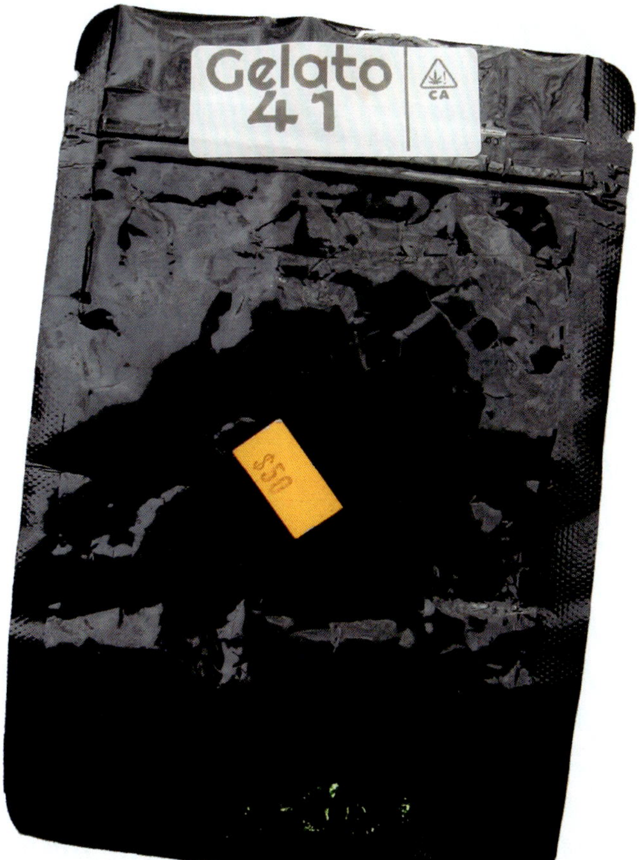
Gelato 41
CA
$50

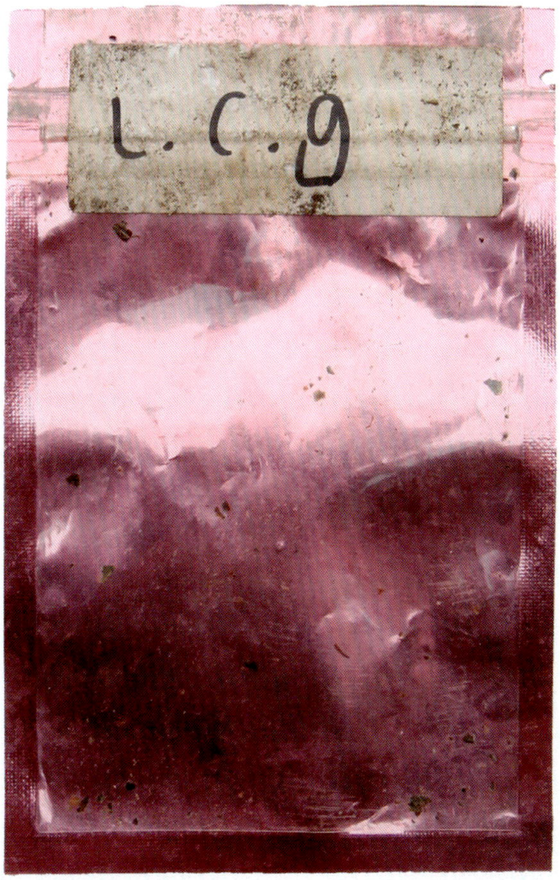
L.C.9

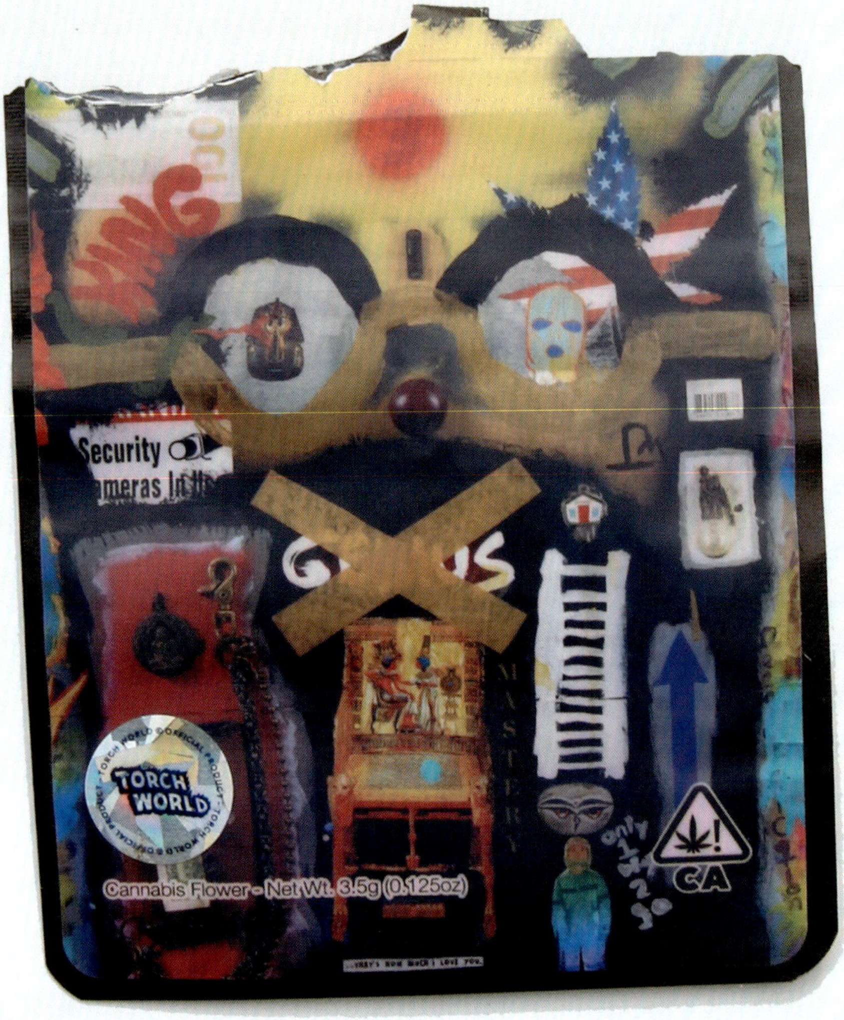

Security
TORCH WORLD
MASTERY
CA
Cannabis Flower - Net Wt. 3.5g (0.125oz)

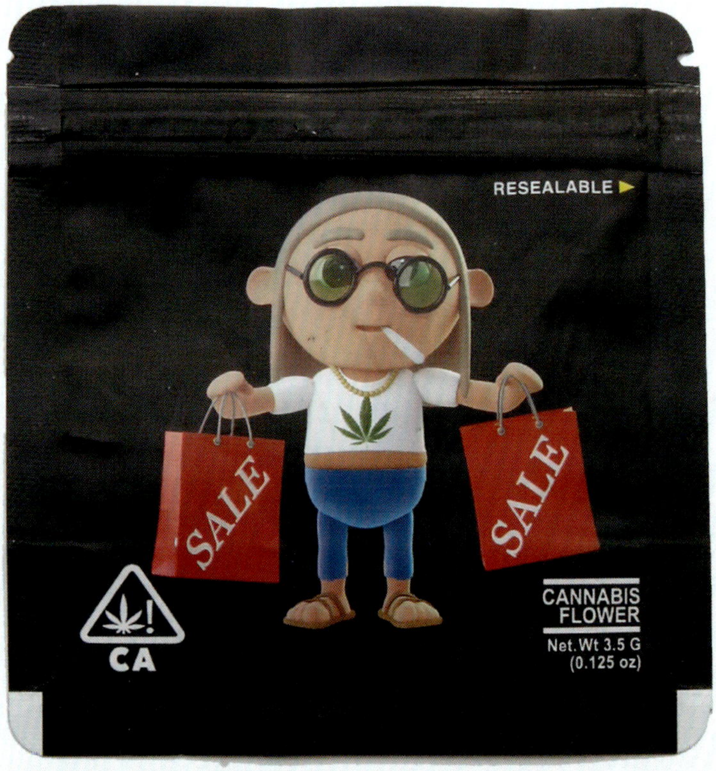

RESEALABLE
SALE
SALE
CA
CANNABIS FLOWER
Net.Wt 3.5 G
(0.125 oz)

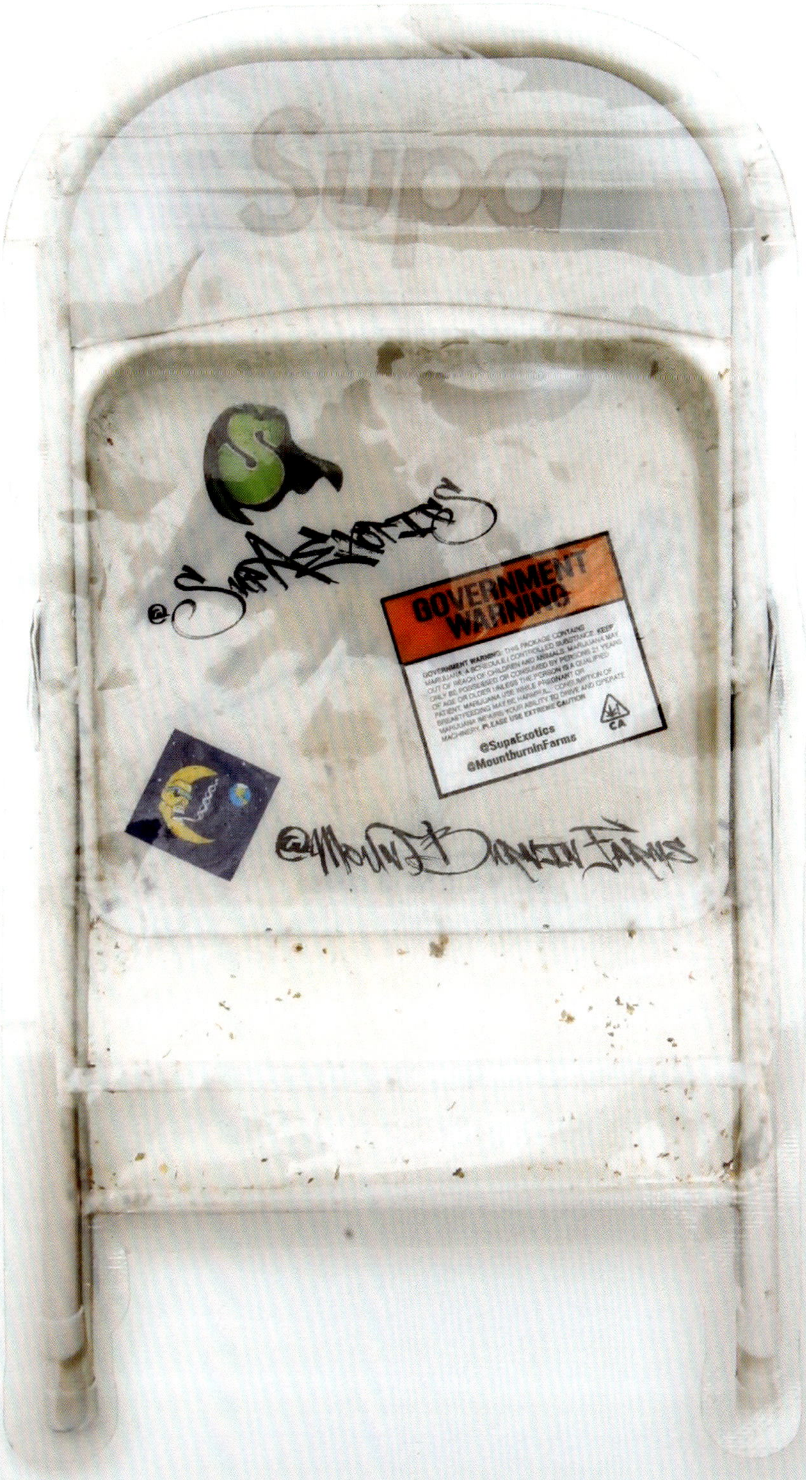
Supa
GOVERNMENT WARNING
@SupaExotics
@MountburnInFarms
CA

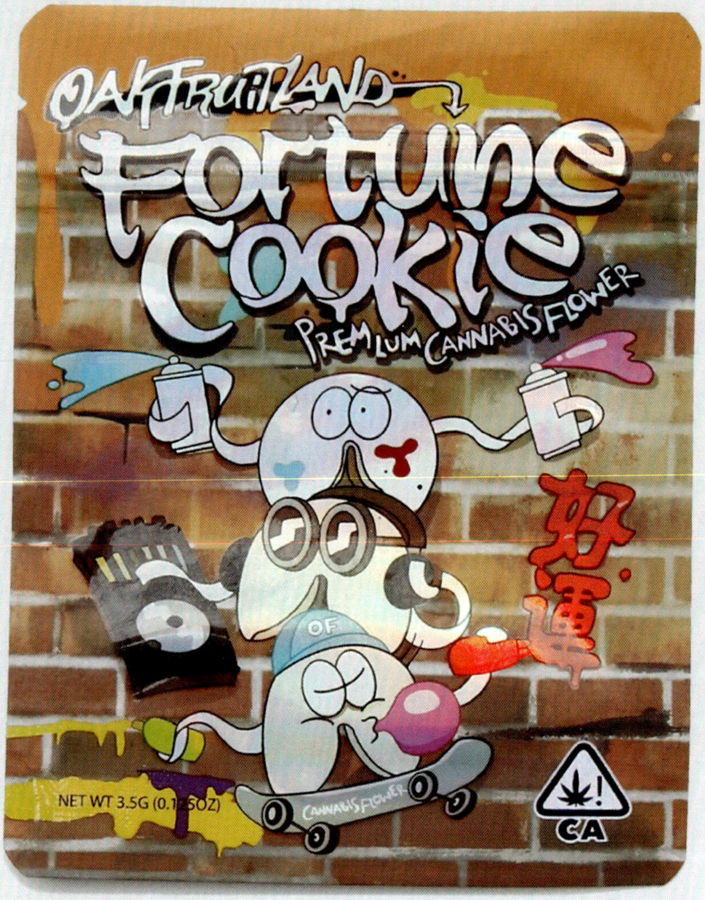
OAKFRUITLAND
Fortune Cookie
CANNABIS FLOWER
好運
OF
CANNABIS FLOWER
NET WT 3.5G
CA

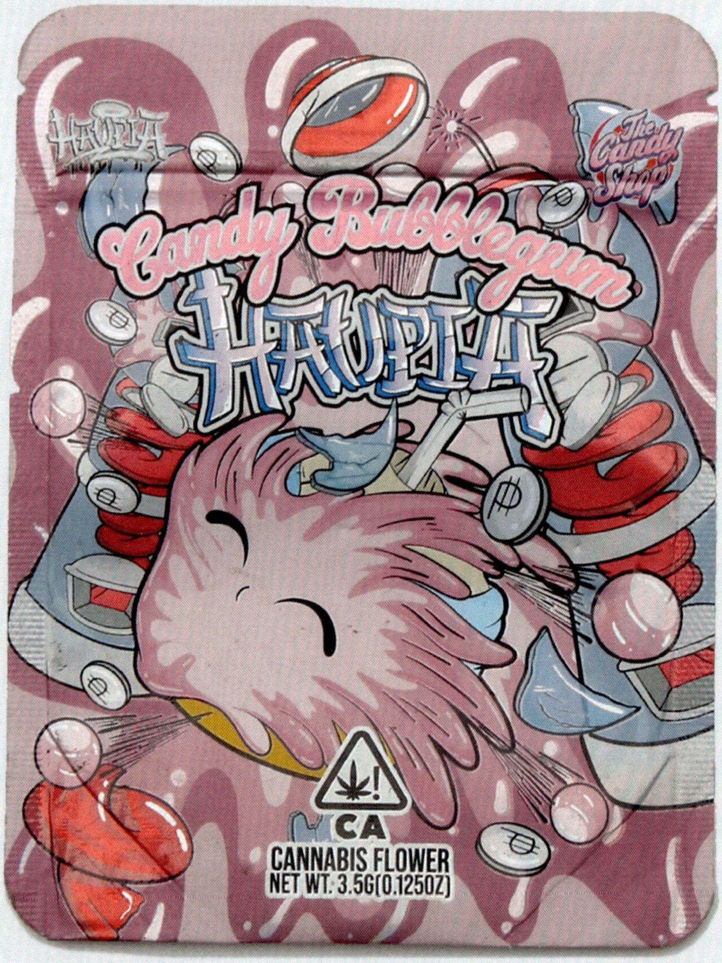
The Candy Shop
Candy Bubblegum
HAUPIA
CA
CANNABIS FLOWER
NET WT. 3.5G(0.125OZ)

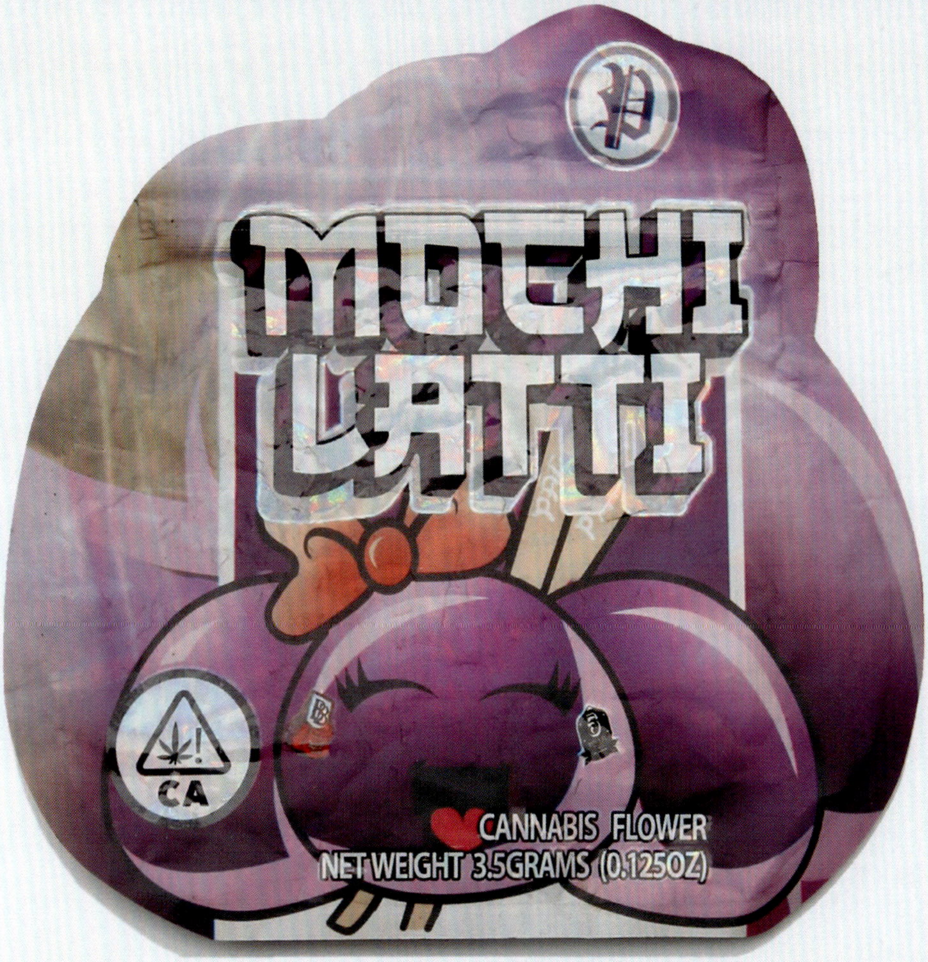
MOCHI LATTI
CANNABIS FLOWER
NET WEIGHT 3.5GRAMS (0.125OZ)

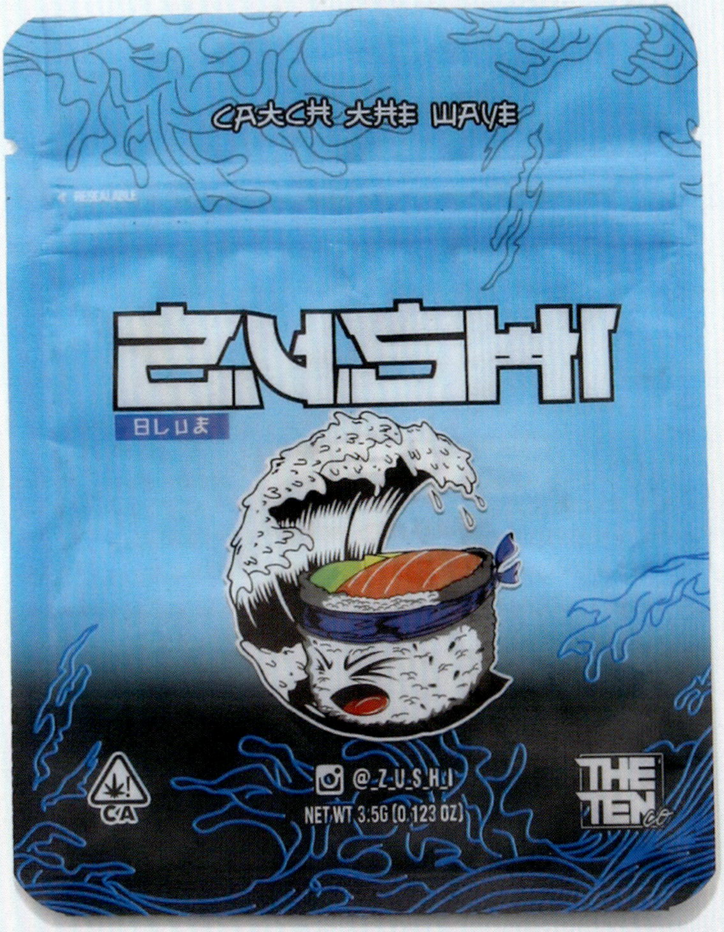
CATCH THE WAVE
ZUSHI
@ZUSHI
NET WT 3.5G (0.123 OZ)
THE TEN

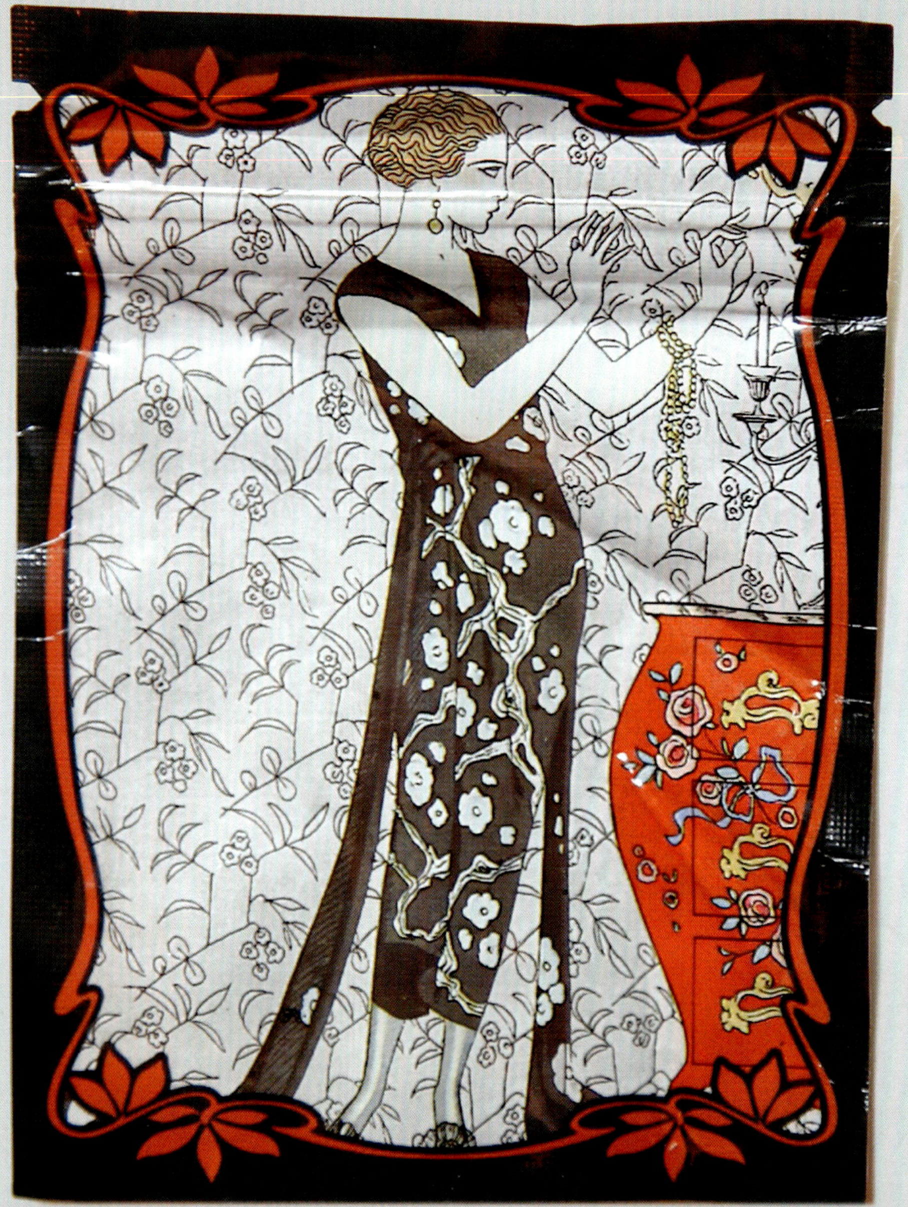

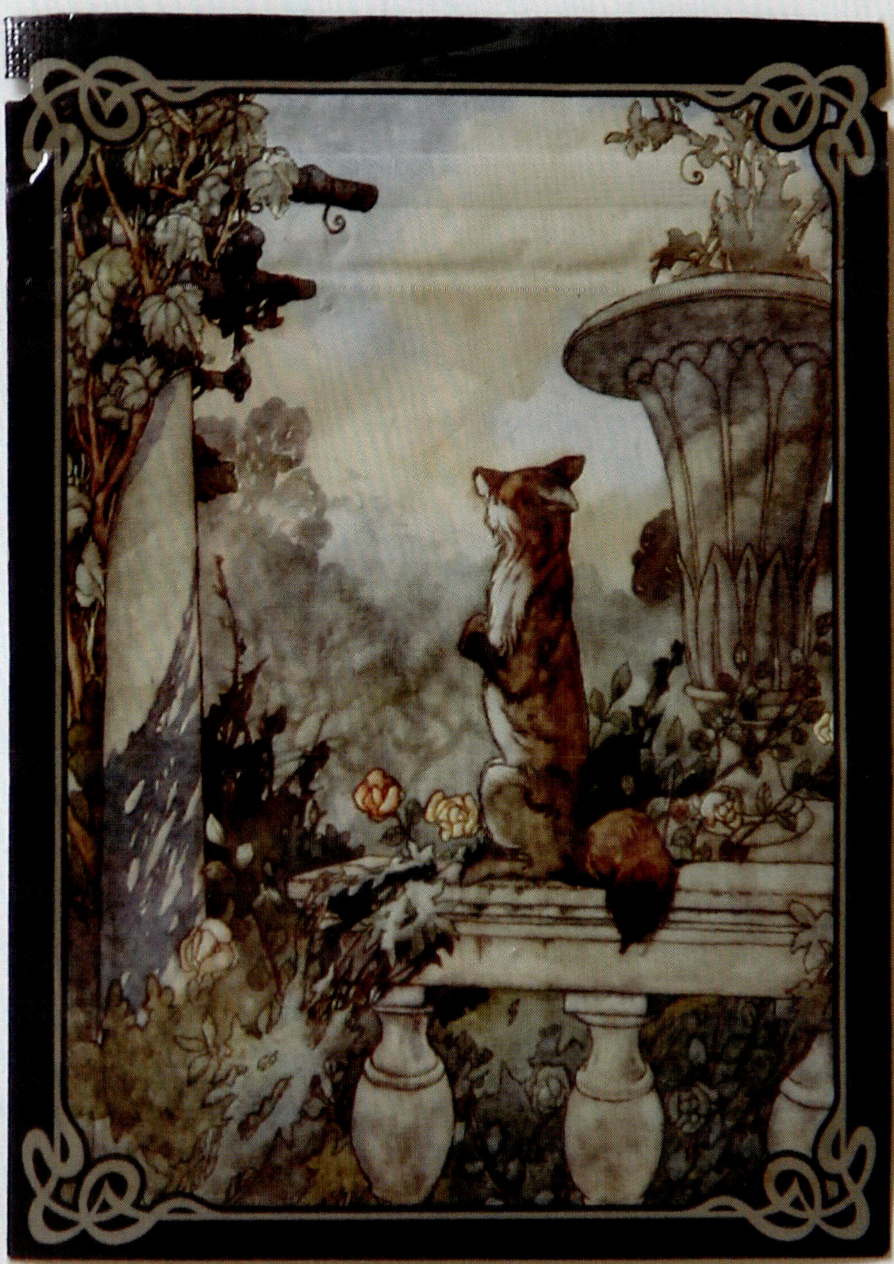

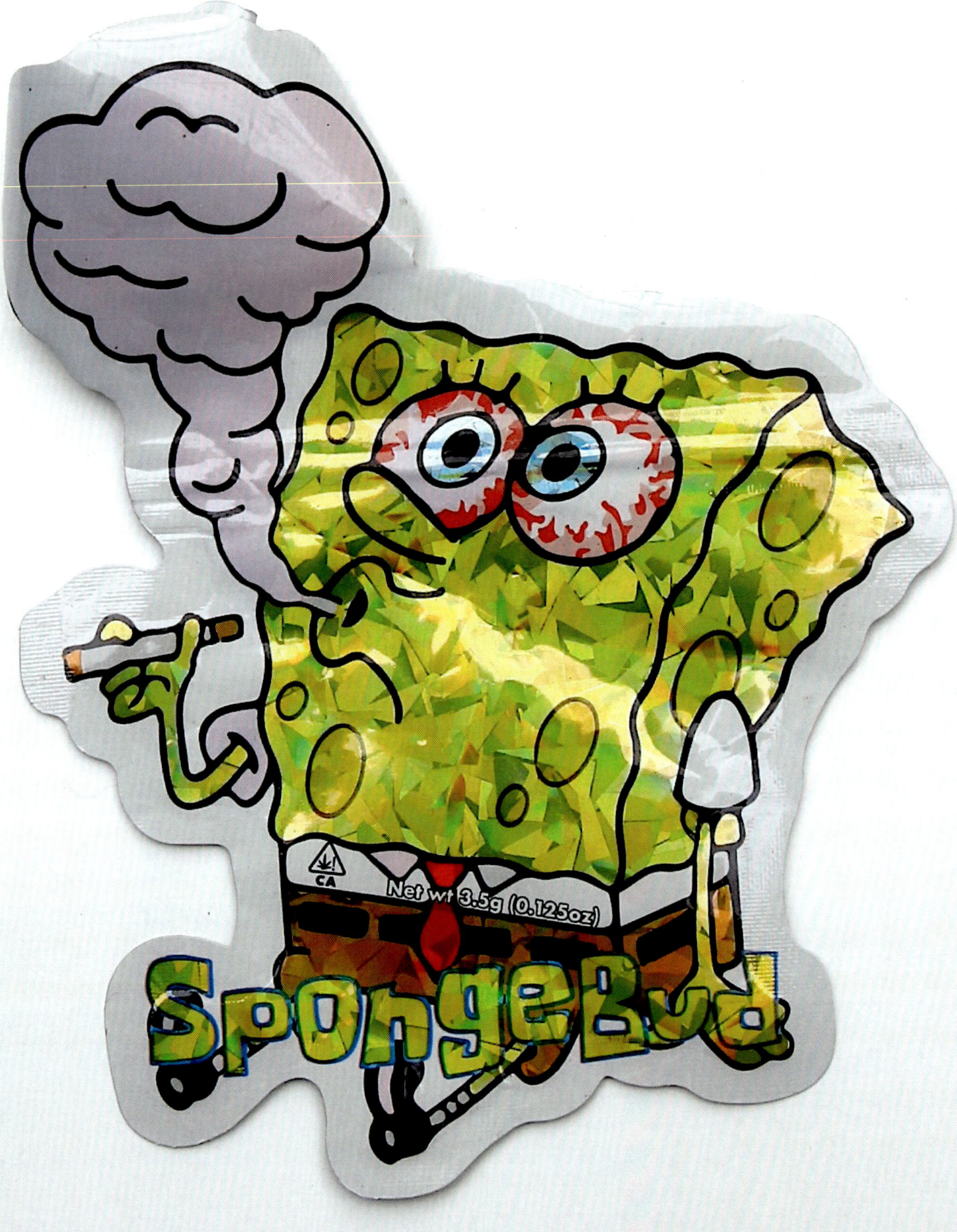
CA
Net wt 3.5g (0.125oz)
SpongeBud

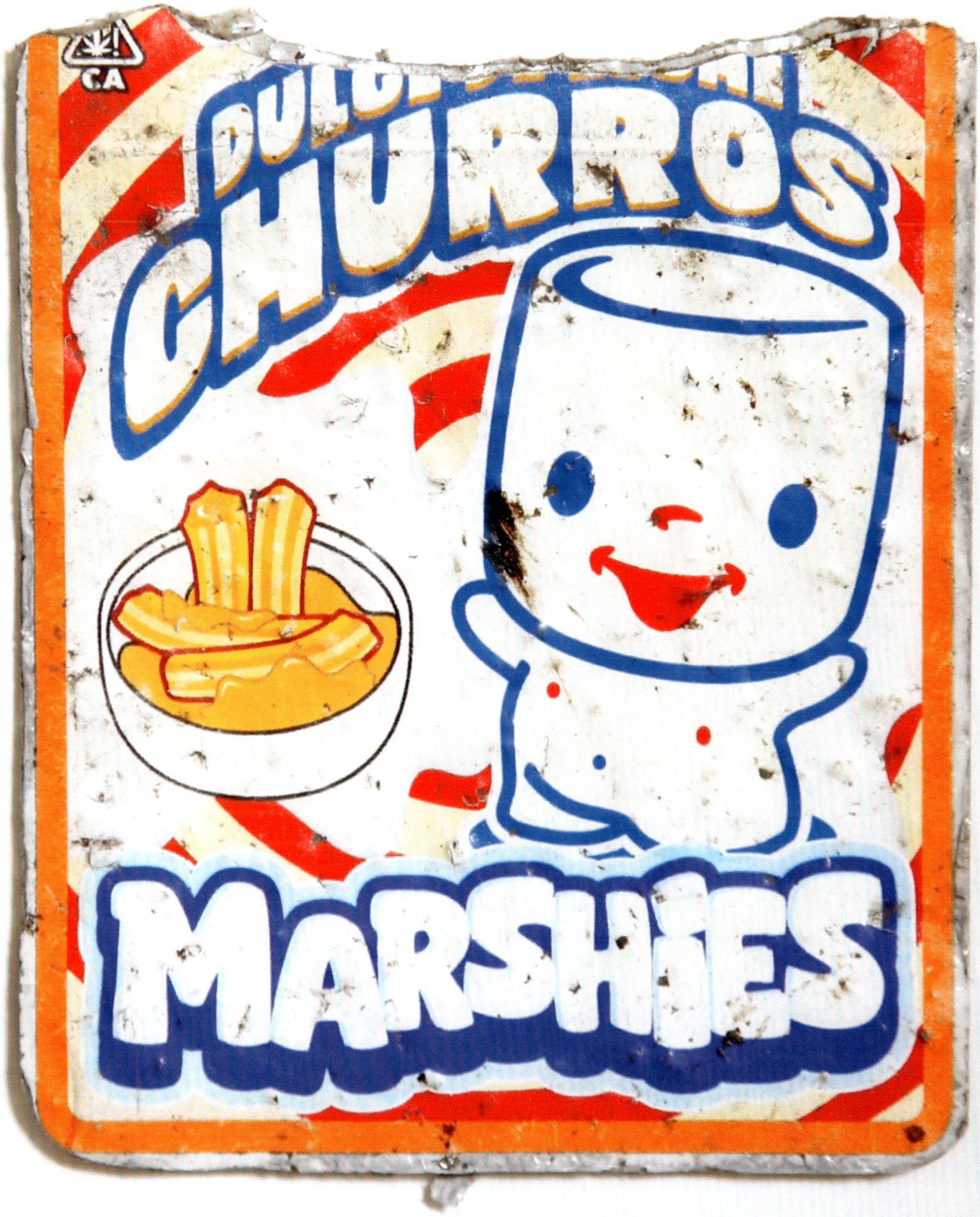
CA
CHURROS
MARSHIES

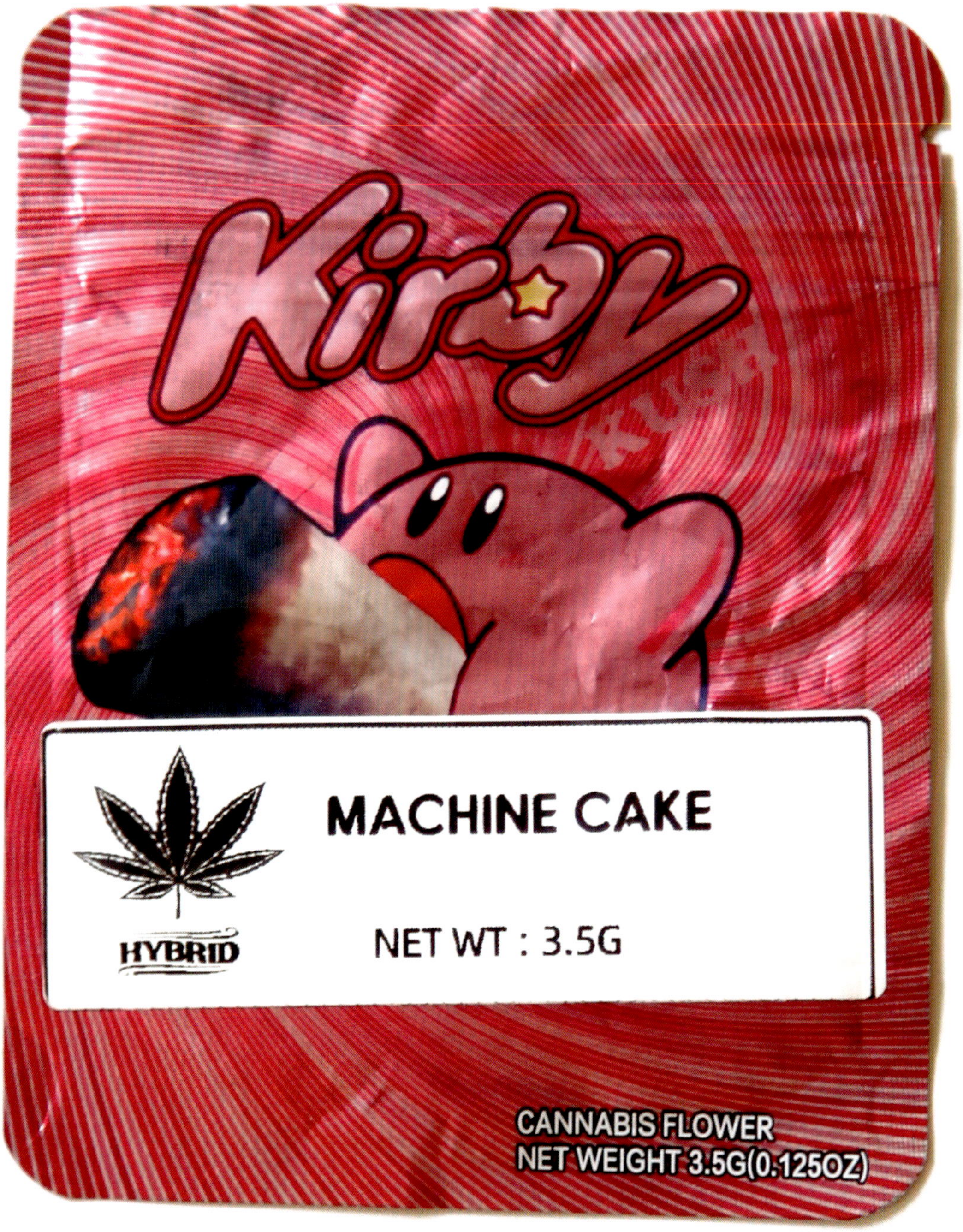
Kirby
KUSH
MACHINE CAKE
HYBRID
NET WT : 3.5G
CANNABIS FLOWER
NET WEIGHT 3.5G(0.125OZ)

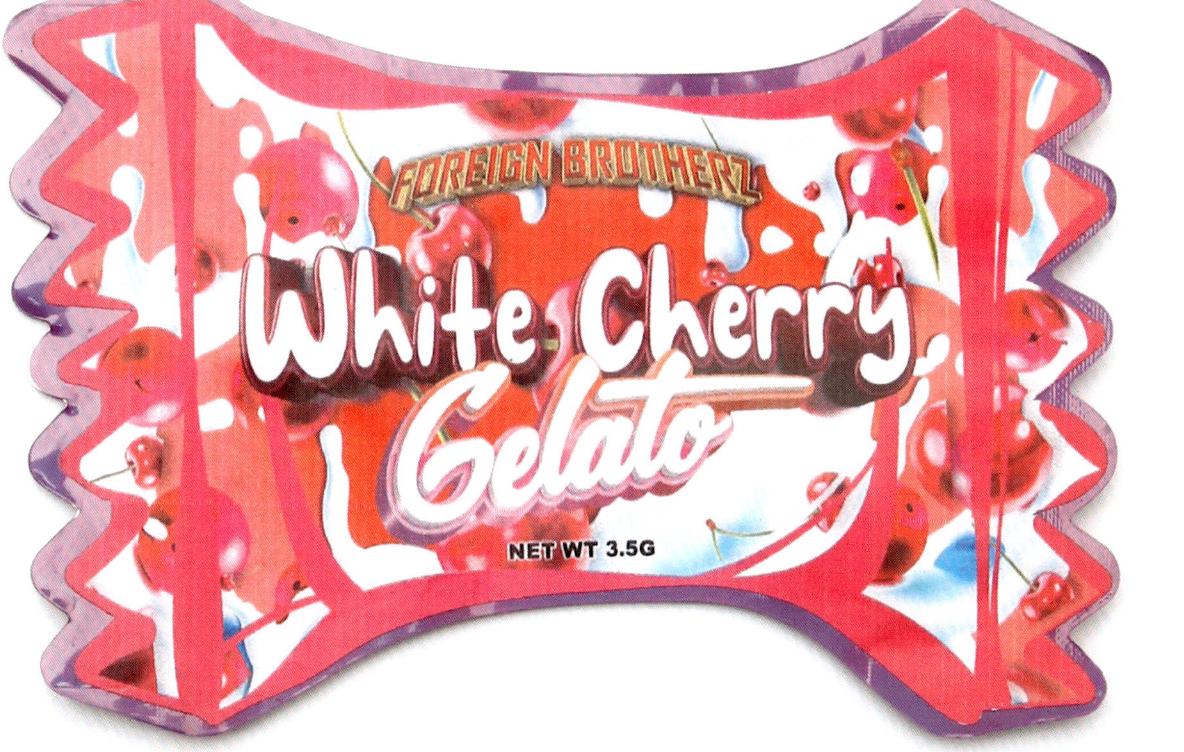

FOREIGN BROTHERZ
White Cherry
Gelato
NET WT 3.5G

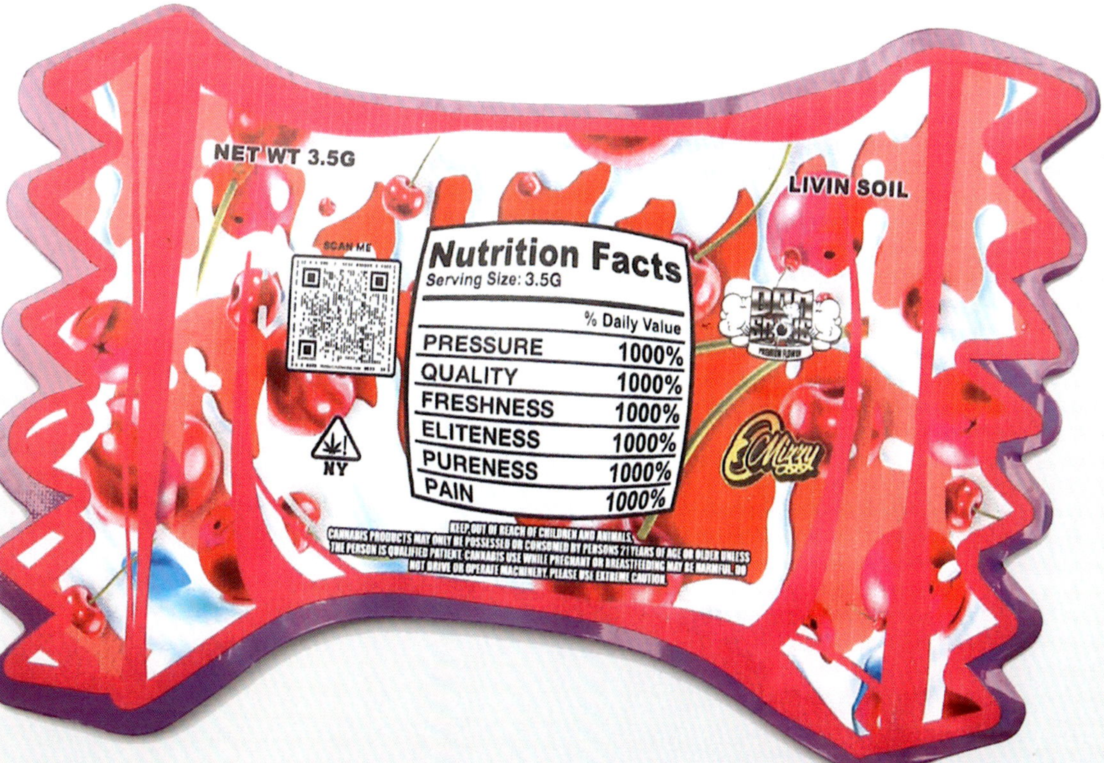

NET WT 3.5G
LIVIN SOIL
SCAN ME
Nutrition Facts
Serving Size: 3.5G
% Daily Value
PRESSURE 1000%
QUALITY 1000%
FRESHNESS 1000%
ELITENESS 1000%
PURENESS 1000%
PAIN 1000%
NY
KEEP OUT OF REACH OF CHILDREN AND ANIMALS.
CANNABIS PRODUCTS MAY ONLY BE POSSESSED OR CONSUMED BY PERSONS 21 YEARS OF AGE OR OLDER UNLESS
THE PERSON IS QUALIFIED PATIENT. CANNABIS USE WHILE PREGNANT OR BREASTFEEDING MAY BE HARMFUL. DO
NOT DRIVE OR OPERATE MACHINERY. PLEASE USE EXTREME CAUTION.

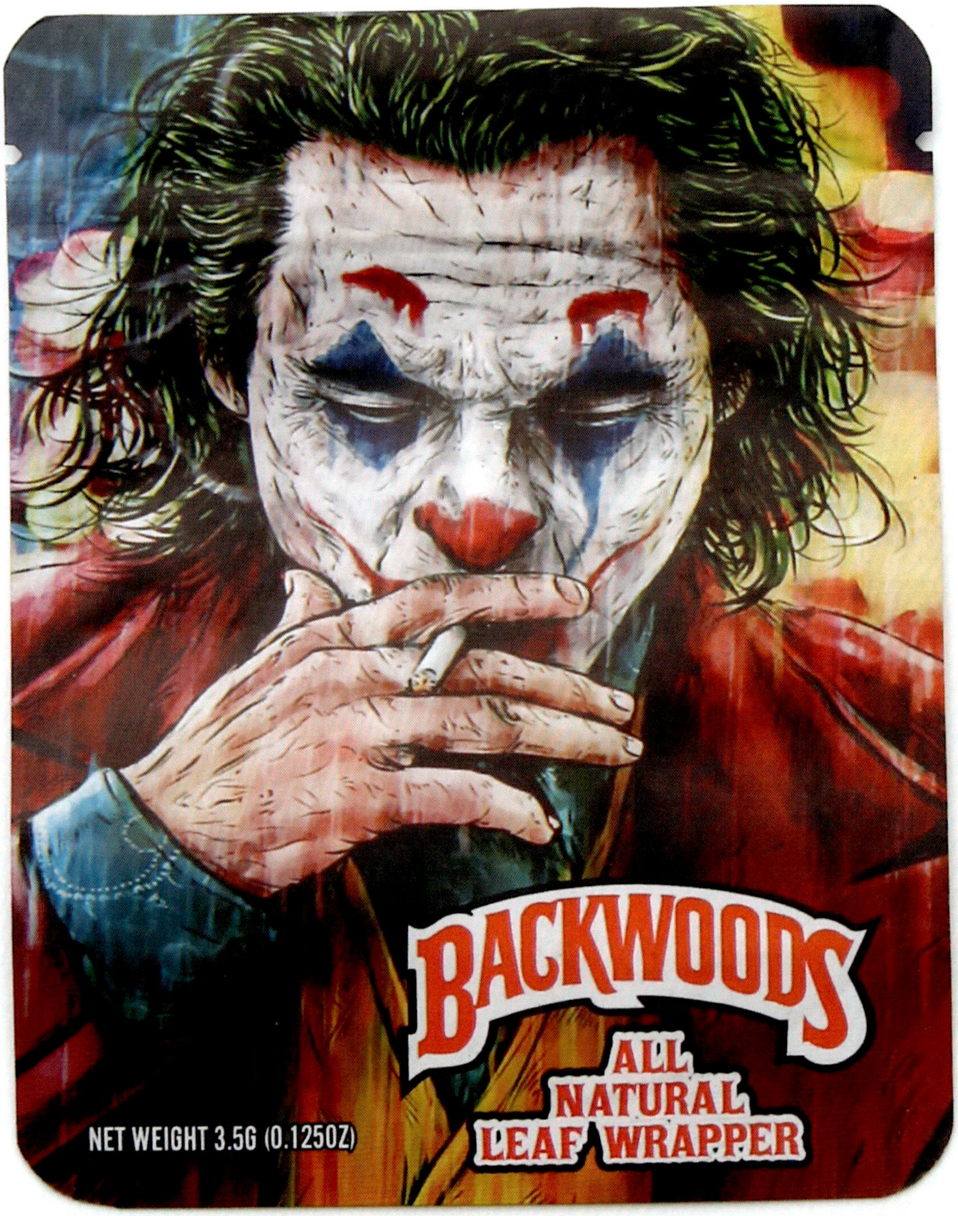
BACKWOODS
ALL
NATURAL
LEAF WRAPPER
NET WEIGHT 3.5G (0.125OZ)

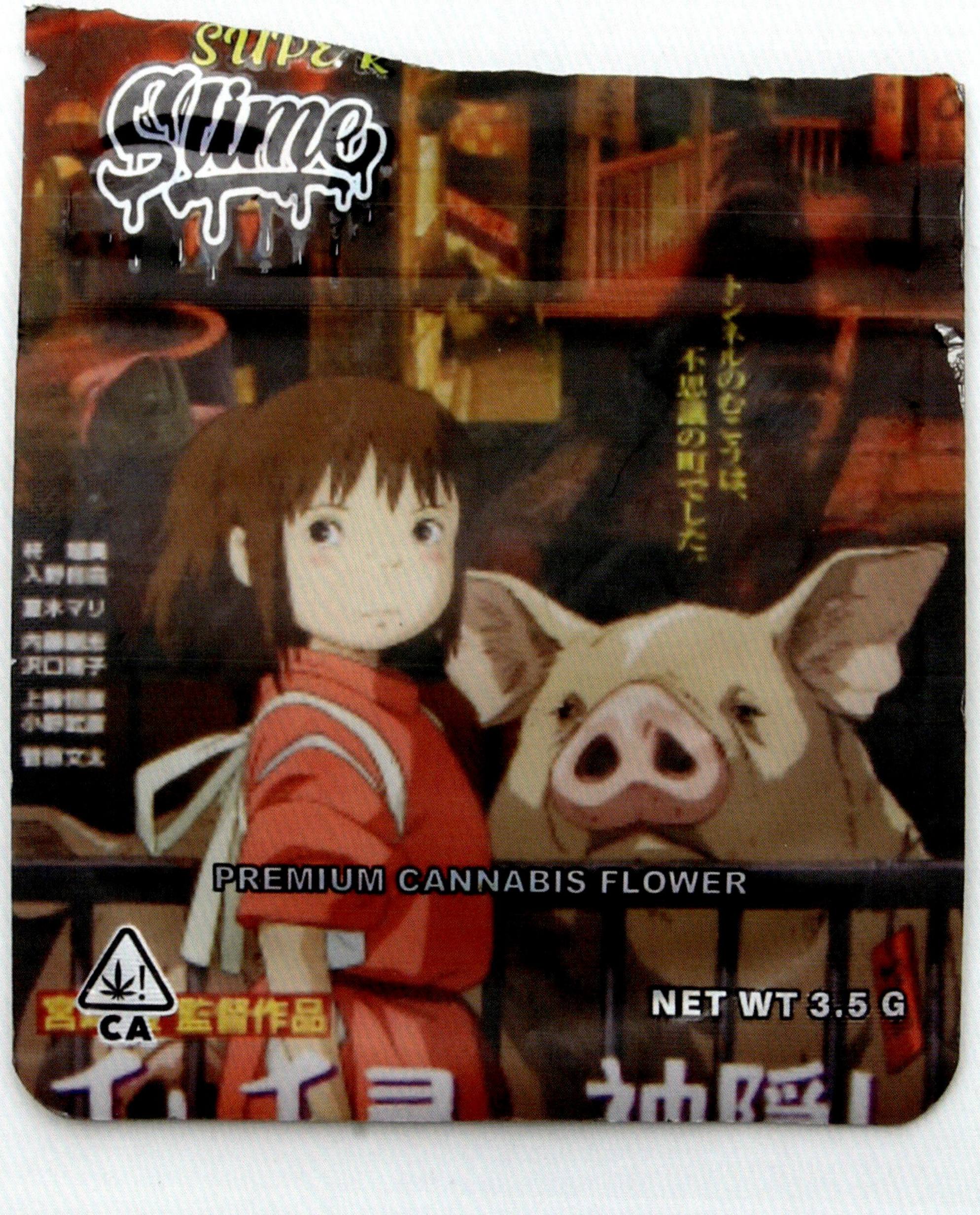
Slime
トンネルのむこうは、
不思議の町でした。
PREMIUM CANNABIS FLOWER
CA
監督作品
NET WT 3.5 G

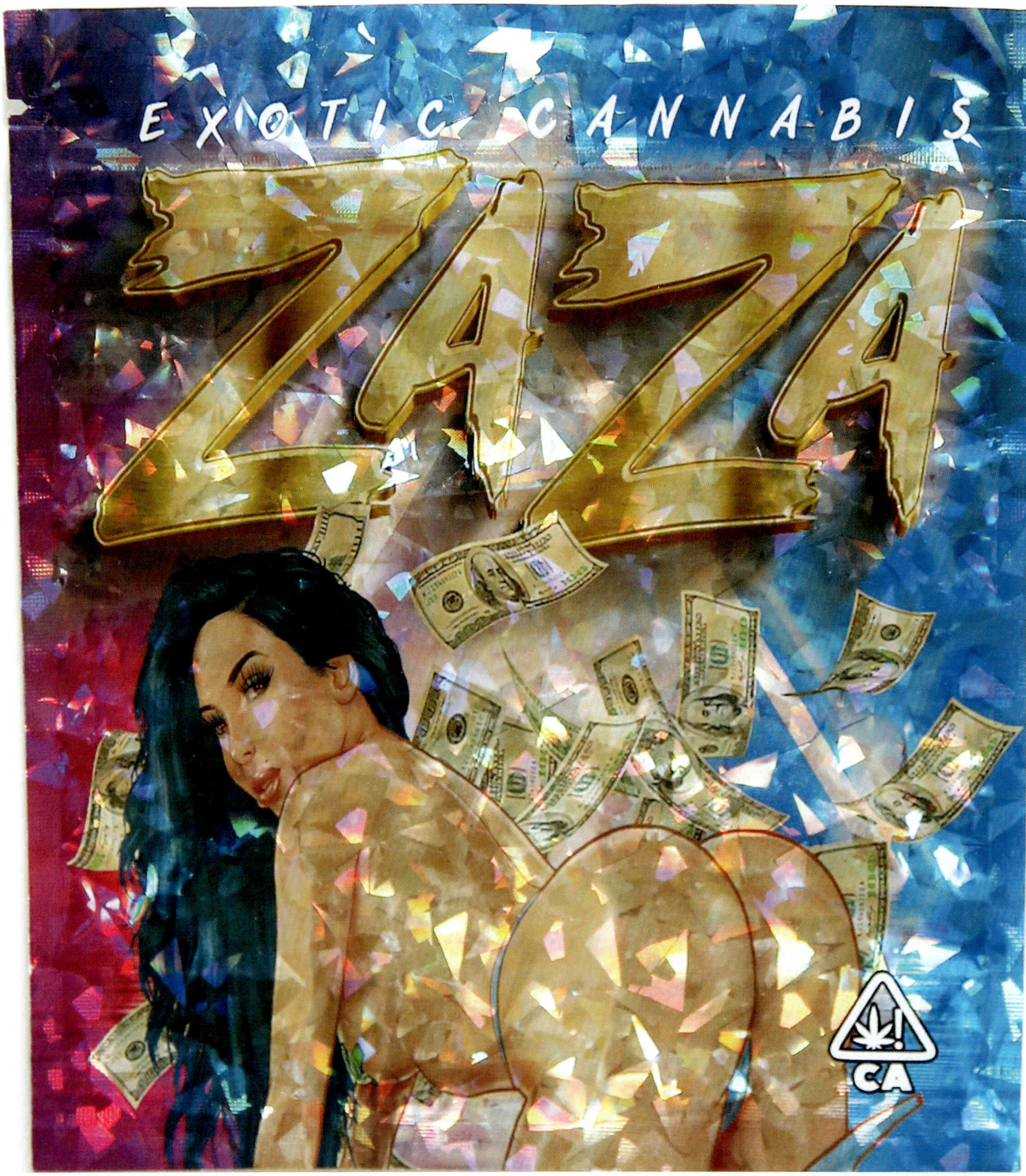
EXOTIC CANNABIS
ZAZA
CA

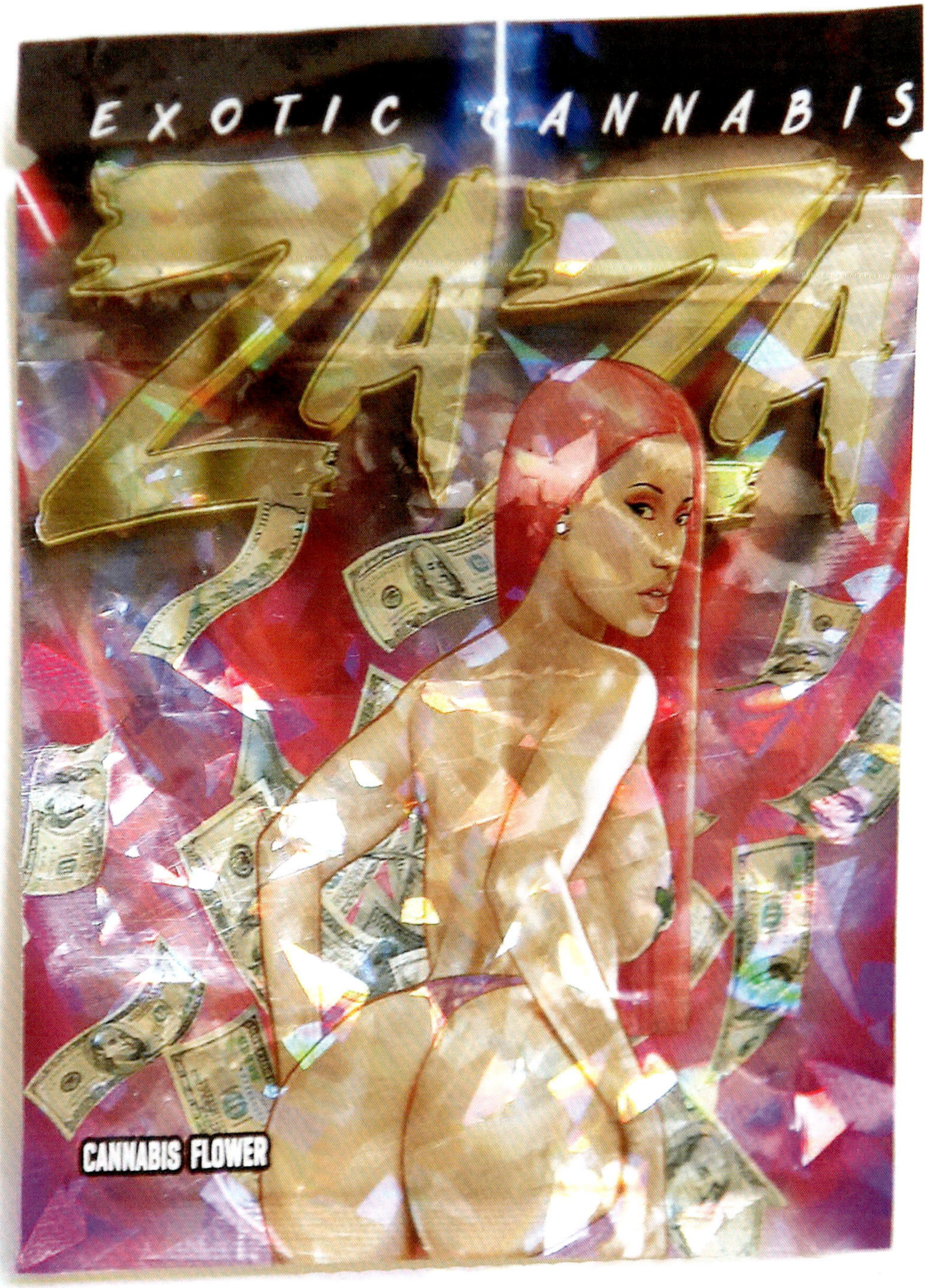
EXOTIC CANNABIS
ZAZA
CANNABIS FLOWER

Za Zine
A collection of weed bags found in New York City
November 2023 to February 2024

Louis Bubko
@foundbylouis
www.bylouis.org

Published by Blurring Books
@blurringbooksnyc
www.blurringbooks.com

Project Management
Sean M. Johnson

First Edition,
Second printing

Design by Louis Bubko

Number 14 in the Blurring Books LSP Series